This page intentionally left blank

An Introduction to the West Wirral Coastline

Written by Tony Franks-Buckley

The name Wirral is derived from the Gaelic meaning "Wyre Heal" or "Myrtle Corner". This is because of the peninsula being heavily forested in the past. The area was populated by large amounts of deer and other game, so much so that in medieval times kings and noblemen used the area for hunting. The emblem of Wirral is the Wirral Horn. The Horn is a brass tipped hunting horn used by the foresters of Wirral and is portrayed in many of the Coats of Arms associated with the peninsula. The horn was given to Alan Sylvester... the first Forrester of Wirral and has passed through thirty generations to the present owner... the Honourable Vivian Baring who has leant it to Wirral Museums where it has been on display.

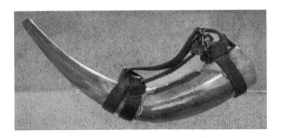

The Wirral Horn & the Wirral Coat of Arms, features the Wirral Horn attached to the trident on the green shield

3

Dedication

This book is dedicated to all my friends and family who have supported me through my life and help me achieve the goals that I have reached. I also dedicate it to my loved ones who are gone but not forgotten.

Acknowledgements

I would like to thank my family who have supported me through tough times and good times especially my Mum and my best friend Uncle John. I would also like to thank those that have educated me and allowed me to become the person that I am today. And last but not least I would like to thank Gavin Chappell whose previous work on Pirates in the area has helped me considerably as well as the help he has also given me.

About the Author

Wallasey Historian and Author that completed BA Honours Degree in Modern History at Liverpool John Moores University under the guidance of fellow author Prof Frank McDonough, Dr Mike Benbough-Jackson and a host of others.

Main interests in history are from the Industrial Revolution era in Britain, which was the beginning of the modern day Britain as we know it today. Also holds a keen interest in World War II due to being taught about the war through Uncle, who served in the Royal Navy and was involved in the D-Day landings.

As well as graduating from university, previously attended Wirral Metropolitan College in Birkenhead and gained A Level results through an Access to Higher Education Diploma in English Literature, History and Environmental Studies which allowed advancement to University

Introduction to Wirral

The name Wirral occurs in the Anglo-Saxon Chronicle as *"Wirheal"*. This literally means "myrtle-corner" from the Old English wir, a myrtle tree, and heals, an angle, corner or slope. It is supposed that the land was once overgrown with bog myrtle, a plant no longer found in the area but plentiful around Formby, to which Wirral would once have provided a similar habitat. The name was given to the Hundred of Wirral around the 8th century, although by the time of the *Doomsday Book* and for some time afterwards the name of the hundred changed to the Hundred of Wilaveston, which later became Willaston.

The earliest evidence of human occupation of Wirral dates from the Mesolithic period, around 7000 BC. Excavations at Greasby have uncovered flint tools and signs of stake holes and a hearth used by a hunter-gatherer community, and other evidence from about the same period has been found at Irby, Hoylake and New Brighton. Later Neolithic stone axes have been found at several locations including Oxton, Neston, and Meols, where Neolithic pottery has also been found. At Meols and New Brighton there is evidence of continuing occupation through to the Bronze Age, around 1000 BC, and funerary urns of the period have been found at West Kirby and Hilbre. Before the time of the Romans, Wirral was inhabited by a Celtic tribe, the Cornovii. Discoveries of artefacts at Meols suggest that it was an important port from at least as early as 500 BC. Traders came from as far away as Gaul and the Mediterranean in search of minerals from North Wales and Cheshire. There are also remains of a small Iron Age fort at Burton, which takes its name (*burh-tún*) from it.

A Subsidy Roll of 1545 shows that the total population of Wirral at the time was no more than 4,000. The peninsula was divided into about 15 parishes (Wallasey, Bidston, Upton, Woodchurch, West Kirby, Thurstaston, Heswall, Bebington, Bromborough, Eastham, Neston, Burton, Shotwick, Backford and Stoke). Most of these were divided into smaller townships, of which the largest in terms of population were Neston, Burton, Wallasey, Tranmere (then within the parish of Bebington) and Liscard. However, none of these were more than small rural villages.

Wirral's proximity to the port of Chester influenced the history of the Dee side of the peninsula. From about the 14th century, Chester provided facilities for trade with Ireland, Spain, and Germany, and seagoing vessels would "lay to" in the Dee awaiting favourable winds and tides. As the Dee started to silt up, harbouring facilities developed at Shotwick, Burton, Neston, Parkgate, Dawpool, and "Hoyle Lake" or Hoylake. However, there was not a gradual progression of development, and downstream anchorages such as that at Hoyle Lake (which replaced Meols) were in occasional use from medieval times, depending on the weather and state of the tide. The main port facilities were at Neston and Parkgate.

At the same time, the use of larger ships and the growth of commerce and industry in Lancashire started to lead to the growth of Liverpool. The first wet dock in Britain was opened in Liverpool in 1715, and the town's population grew from some 6,000 to 80,000 during the 18th century. The need to develop and protect the port led to a chain of lighthouses being built along the north Wirral coast. The commercial expansion of Liverpool, and the increase in stage coach traffic from Chester, also spurred the growth of ferries across the River Mersey. By the end of the 18th century the Wirral side of the Mersey had five ferry houses, at Seacombe, Woodside, the Rock, New Ferry and Eastham.

Other communications were also improving. Turnpike roads linking Chester with Eastham, Woodside, and Neston were built after 1787. In 1793, work began on the Ellesmere Canal, connecting the River Mersey with Chester and Shropshire through the fluvioglacial landform known as the Backford gap, and the town of Ellesmere Port began to develop.

The excavation of the New Cut of the Dee, opened in 1737, to improve access to Chester, diverted the river's course to the Welsh side of the estuary and took trade away from the Wirral coastline. Although plans were made to overcome its gradual silting up, including one in 1857 to cut a ship canal from a point between Thurstaston and Heswall to run along the length of Wirral to Chester, this and other schemes came to nothing, and the focus of general trade moved irrevocably to the much deeper Mersey. However, from the late 18th century there was coal mining near Neston, in tunnels stretching up to two miles under the Dee, and a Quay at Denhall was used for coal exports.

The Nineteenth Century

The first steam ferry service across the Mersey started in 1817, and steam-powered ships soon opened up Wirral's Mersey coast for participation in industrialisation that was occurring in Britain. The 1820s saw the birth of the area's renowned shipbuilding tradition when John Laird opened his shipyard in Birkenhead, later expanded by his son William. The Lairds were largely responsible for the early growth of Birkenhead, commissioning the architect James Gillespie Graham to lay it out as a new town modelled on Edinburgh. In 1847, Birkenhead's first docks and its municipal park, the first in Britain and the inspiration for New York's Central Park, were opened, and the town expanded rapidly. Birkenhead's population of less than one thousand in 1801 rose to over 33,000 by 1851, and to 157,000 by 1901. The town became a borough in 1877, incorporating within it Oxton, and Tranmere.

The improved communications also allowed Liverpool merchants to buy up and develop large estates in Wirral. James Atherton and William Rowson developed the resort of New Brighton, and new estates for the gentry were also built at Egremont, Oxton, Claughton and Rock Ferry. Arrowe Hall was built for the Shaw family in 1835.

The mid 19th century saw the establishment of docks at Birkenhead and in the Wallasey Pool, and continuing development for a wide range of industry both there and along the banks of the Mersey. The New Chester Road was opened in 1833. Wirral's first railway was built in 1840, planned by George Stephenson and connecting Birkenhead with Chester. In 1852 Price's Patent Candle Company built a factory and model village at Bromborough. This was followed in 1888 by William Lever's establishment of the much larger Sunlight soap factory and Port Sunlight garden village, designed to house its employees and provide them with a benign environment. The opening of the Manchester Ship Canal in 1894, with its outfall at Eastham, led to further port-side and industrial development beside the Mersey at Ellesmere Port.

In 1886, the Mersey Railway tunnel was opened, linking Wirral and Liverpool. This led to the further rapid growth of suburbs along its lines in Wirral, particularly in Wallasey, Hoylake and West Kirby, and later Bebington and Heswall. Wallasey's population grew to over 53,000 by 1901, and the town also achieved borough status soon after the turn of the century

The Twentieth century

The dockland areas of Wallasey and Birkenhead continued to develop and prosper in the first half of the century, specialising in trade with Africa and the Far East. A host of other port-related industries then came into existence, such as flour milling, tanning, edible oil refining and the manufacture of paint and rubber-based products. In 1922 a new oil dock was built at Stanlow near Ellesmere Port, and in 1934 oil refining began there. A large chemical and oil refining complex still dominates the area.

In 1929, the 3rd World Scout Jamboree was held at Arrowe Park and this celebrated the 21st Anniversary of the publication of Scouting for Boys. Thirty-five countries were represented by 30,000 Scouts, plus another 10,000 British Scouts who took the opportunity to camp in the vicinity.

The rail tunnel under the Mersey was supplemented by a vehicle tunnel in 1934, the Queensway Tunnel. A third tunnel opened in 1971, the Kingsway Tunnel, connecting with the M53 motorway which now runs up the centre of the peninsula. These new roads contributed to the massive growth of commuting by car between Liverpool and Wirral, and the development of new suburban estates around such villages as Moreton, Upton, Greasby, Pensby, and Bromborough.

In 1940-41, as part of The Blitz, parts of Wirral, especially around the docks, suffered extensive bomb damage. There were 464 people killed in Birkenhead and 355 in Wallasey, and 80% of all houses in Birkenhead were either destroyed or badly damaged During the Second World War Wirral held two RAF sites, RAF West Kirby (which was a camp, not an airfield) and RAF Hooton Park and a number of anti-aircraft sites in order to protect the docks of Birkenhead and Liverpool.

After the Second World War, economic decline began to set in Birkenhead, as elsewhere in the area which had started to become known as Merseyside. However, there continued to be industrial development along the Mersey between Birkenhead and Ellesmere Port, including the large Vauxhall Motors car factory on the site of RAF Hooton Park.

The major urban centres of Wirral are to its east; these include Birkenhead and Wallasey. To the west and south, Wirral is more rural. Two thirds of the populations of Wirral live on one third of the land - in Birkenhead and Wallasey, according to Wirral Metropolitan Borough Council. Other towns to the south and west of this area are usually considered part of Wirral; notably, Ellesmere Port is often described as one of its 'border towns'. For regional economic planning, The Wirral is considered part of the Liverpool City Region.

West Kirby

West Kirby

The name West Kirby is of Viking origin. The Kirby word was originally pronounced "Kirkjubyr" and means "village with a church". However at that time there was already a place called "Kirkjubyr", and that place was on the other side of the Wirral in Wallasey. In order to differentiate the villages the Norse added the "West", as it was West of Wallasey.

The old village was located around St. Bridget's Church which played a large role in the expansion of West Kirby, however today; the town is centred on West Kirby railway station, which is an estimated half a mile away. At the time of the Doomsday Survey, West Kirby was originally owned by Robert De Rodelent (Rhuddlan in Wales). The survey shows 5 tenements and a Frenchman with a Sergeant and 2 ploughs.

The settlement was in an ideal position it had good farm land, an abundance of fresh water and wildlife, woods, scrubs and marshes as well as hills that looked across the surrounding lands and rivers and had complete access to the River Dee. Many people do not know that several centuries ago, West Kirby was an island just like Wallasey. Given its strategic location at the mouth of the Dee just across from Point of Ayr in North Wales it is little wonder why maritime history is so prevalent in the West Kirby area. The Dee today is much different to the River of over 1000 years ago. Back in the early centuries, large vessels could go into the River Dee until they reached the marsh land of Thingwall or Dingsmere, however today much of the Dee Estuary is silting up and needs constant maintenance.

Promenade, West Kirby

West Kirby is also famous for its Victorian promenade, flanked by the Marine Lake that permits boats to sail even at low tide. In the Victorian days West Kirby was a great sea side town, much like New Brighton as mentioned in my previous book. It had fine sandy beaches, many shops and a large variety of hotels and entertainment including children's and adults activities. Many early photographs shows the beaches packed with family's sporting large pants and shirts, the woman were well covered with large hats and the children with long pants seen building sand castles. Donkey rides were also great entertainment and many were available to pace up and down the beach front. Just like today, a short walk whilst the tide was out allowed a day trip to Hilbre Island and was always a hit for the more curious day trippers. The beaches were also packed with entertainers, hawkers and punch and Judy shows for the kids, a true picture of a Victorian seaside resort.

The West Kirby marine lake was opened in 1899 at 1000 meters long and 140 meters wide, it was a great place to try out ever more popular water activities. In the 1980s the lake suffered a catastrophic leak and as a result a new lake was constructed on the site which is wider than previous and allows for more sporting activities. The lake still exists today and after the creation of West Kirby Sailing Club in 1901 it has proved a huge increase to the village's revenue and ensures that West Kirby has the largest amount of members in Merseyside.

In October 1991 the World Wind surfing Speed Record was set on the Marine Lake at 42.16 knots. It was held for 2 years until it was beaten in Australia. Grange Hill commands great views of the River Dee. The outstanding position of the hill was noticed at an early time by mariners and as such a sandstone column with a ball on top was placed on the summit of the hill as a beacon for mariners. The hill had originally been home to a large windmill which had also been used as a land mark by passing mariners. The column was erected as a beacon only after the windmill was blow down on the 6th January 1839, which saw sailors struggle to navigate.

The Hoylake and West Kirby War Memorial as seen above is another notable local landmark, it was designed in 1922 by the British sculptor "Charles Sargeant Jagger", who was responsible for a number of war memorials around the world, including the Royal Artillery Memorial at Hyde Park Corner in London.

Charles Sargeant Jagger MC (1885-1934) was a British sculptor who, following active service in the First World War, sculpted many works on the theme of war. He is best known for his war memorials and his memories and experience during WW1 is said to show in his prolific sculptures which he designs.

The memorial at West Kirby stands at the summit of Grange Hill overlooking the surrounding area, its huge shaft rising high into the air above the town. It is a large imposing stone obelisk which was built to show those lost during the Great War that they have not given their life in vain.

Location

On Grange Hill, overlooking West Kirby, Cheshire.
Access via a footpath from Homestead Mews.

**IN GRATITUDE TO GOD AND
TO THE MEN AND WOMEN FROM
THESE PARTS WHO LAID DOWN
THEIR LIVES IN THE GREAT WAR
1914 - 1919 - 1939 - 1945
THEY WERE A WALL UNTO US
BOTH BY NIGHT AND DAY.**

On two sides of the obelisk stand bronze figures symbolising war
and peace. On the west face is a figure of a robed woman holding a
baby, a wreath of poppies and broken manacles. On the east face
stands a British infantry soldier dressed for winter and standing
guard with standard issue .303 rifle with a bayonet fixed, a gas

mask, water bottle, putties and his helmet pushed off the back of his head, and a German helmet at his feet.

Behind West Kirby Marine Lake their used to stand a large imposing hotel (See Above), built in circa 1890 and extended in 1896, it was named "The Hydropathic Hotel", but known locally as 'The Hydro' for short. The hotel seen above was first lit by candles.

At the south end of the Marine Lake, which is now integrated into a modern house, there is a small circular sandstone tower. The tower is known as 'Tell's Tower'. It was built by John Cumming Mcdona M.P in memory of a remarkable St. Bernhard dog for which he had great affection for. John Cumming Macdona lived at Hilbre House in West Kirby with his dog. After the animal died in 1871 he built the tower in the corner of his garden as seen below.

He buried the dog underneath with a plaque and small inscription as a dedication to his beloved pet. The entrance to Tell's Tower can be seen from Riverside, and the actual tower can be seen from the slipway down to the river Dee.

The Macdonas, were a family from Ireland. William Coules Macdona became vicar of St. Marks in Royton, Nr. Oldham and the benefactor of the land to the church was his older brother John Cumming Macdona who for a time was MP for Rotherhithe. He too was a reverend at some time in his life and also he was president of the Kennel Club. John Cumming Macdona lived in Hilbre House in West Kirby. The family are now all dead, the last of them was Mrs Macdona was alive in the 1960s or 70s. The Macdonas gave the land for the use of the West Kirby sailing club and where Macdona drive is now situated, was where their house was.

West Kirby Sailing School

With thanks to the sailing school for collaborating the information. All credit goes to them.

West Kirby Sailing Club was formed in 1901 and has grown into one of the largest sailing clubs in the UK. It all started in the Hydropathic Hotel, a building which has since been demolished and replaced with the Hilbre Court. A small group of gentlemen wanted to form a club from which to sail on the recently built marine lake. WKSC was born.

In the early days West Kirby Sailing Club met in a room in the hotel before moving into a club house and raced on the marine lake in 12ft dinghies.

In **1948** the first Wilson Trophy took place, it was then named the YRA Firefly Championships.

In **1953** a new purpose built clubhouse was erected and is still in use today, after many alterations. The new clubhouse would provide changing facilities and a comfortable place in which to run racing from.

In **1985** the marine lake wall which was built in 1899 was breached and it was WKSC members who came to the rescue, coming up with a plan to construct temporary repairs. Hoards of WKSC members took part in this operation and before long the hole in the wall was repaired and racing continued.

Unfortunately the repair didn't last that long, eventually it gave way and plans were drawn up for a new marine lake. The then commodore of the club had to fight hard to get it built and fight even harder to get it to the size it is.

In **1986** West Kirby had its first season with racing only taking place on the River Dee.

In **1987** the new marine lake opened, with new pontoons and new slipways. WKSC also got a massive extension to the boat yard. The membership instantly increased.

In **1988** the inaugural Eric Twiname Championships were held at West Kirby and gave the club a chance to show how much it had grown up. HRH Princess Anne visited the club and presented the prizes to the competitors.

In 1995 the club ran the first IYRU (now ISAF) World Team Racing Championships. It took place over a week during the summer alongside the British Open Team Racing Championships for the Wilson Trophy.

Sailing takes place on the marine lake on weekday evenings between April and October and at weekends from April to December. There is also tidal sailing between April and October.

The Clubhouse opens six nights each week (not Sunday nights) and at lunch time at weekends, Bank Holidays and Wednesdays.

It is Club policy for a whole family to join at the same time whenever possible when children may join from age seven; otherwise they must be over ten. The application procedures are designed to ensure that prospective new members are acquainted with the Club facilities and have had the opportunity to meet members with similar interests to their own before joining. We always aim to be as welcoming and helpful as possible.

Membership categories are grouped into various price bands which take account of different circumstances including age, distance living away from the Club and number of people in household. Those aged over 65 (after 3 years membership) or under 26 can enjoy subscriptions at a reduced rate. We also have an outport membership for those who live a distance away from the Club (defined by postcodes) for more than eight months of the year. Family membership means that only one subscription is payable for all the children in the household aged between 7 and 18

A variety of social functions are arranged for members by the House Committee and details of forthcoming events are displayed on the notice board behind the bar in the Main Room and also on the website. Members may hire rooms for private functions subject to the approval of the General Committee well in advance.

There is a busy programme of events in the winter months including Ship-shape on Tuesdays, a quiz on Wednesdays and Bridge is played in the Wilson Room on Thursdays throughout the year. Each Friday evening is Club night in the Main Room and the 200 Plus Club is held on the last Friday of each month in the Main Room.

The various notice boards around the Club advertise sailing events, social functions and official notices. There are also notice boards in the entrance hall where members may advertise boats for sale and crewing requirements. This is the only unauthorised advertising in the Club. The website is also regularly updated with a wealth of information and photographs. The Club magazine,

Seldom Seen, is published three times a year and is financed by advertising. It is named after a buoy in the Dee Estuary.

<u>Rules & Traditions of the Club:</u>

The General Rules and the Club Handbook are given out on election. Bar opening times, Club Rule 44 (Liability of Club) and the House Regulations are displayed on the Official Notices Board in the rear entrance.

Children under 10 must always be under parental supervision when on Club premises and may use the Main Room at lunch times at weekends or Bank Holidays. Juniors aged 10 to 14 can also use the Main Room on Friday evenings and after bona fide sailing in the week until 9.30 pm and must leave the premises by 10.00pm. Juniors 14 to 18 may normally use the Main Room until 10.30 pm on a Friday except they must vacate by 9.45 pm on the night of the 200 Plus Club. Juniors are not permitted to use the Macdona Room or consume alcohol. Please see House Regulations for full information.

Guests must be signed into the Visitors' Book and may come to the Club a maximum of six times in any one year. Non members aged under 18 must be introduced to a Club Officer and shall be subject to the same Rules as a Junior Member of an equivalent age.

The Club has several traditions. Please remove all headgear when entering the premises. The bell in the Main Room must only be rung for official announcements, when there are a prescribed number of rings for each Officer. The traditional penalty for breaking these rules is drinks all round! Gentlemen (and ladies) are requested not to be bare chested in the Clubhouse.

The Dee Estuary is a tidal and the trot moorings flood approximately two hours forty minutes before high water. Our racing finishes about an hour and a half after high water on an average tide. The height of tide varies and the best racing occurs with a height over eight metres.

There are three tidal moored classes, **Stars, Falcons and Hilbres**, which have organised races, usually at weekends according to the height and time of the tides.

Stars are the Club's senior class and are clinker built (i.e. overlapping planks) and date back originally to 1906. Falcons are similar to a large dinghy and are now mainly of glass fibre construction, although we still have a number of wooden Falcons which remain competitive. Hilbres are heavier clinker built boats with a cuddy (cabin top).

The dinghy classes use the marine lake in the evening during the week and either the tide or lake at weekends. Our dinghy classes comprise **Fireflies** (highly manoeuvrable, 12 foot, 2 sail boats) **GP14s** (14 foot, 3 sail, general purposes dinghies), **Lasers** (nearly 13 foot, glass fibre, single sail dinghies), **Larks** (14 foot, glass fibre, 3 sail dinghies) and **Mirrors** (small gunter rigged dinghies). Exclusively for junior members are the fleets of **Cadets** and **Optimists**. **Cadets** are small 3 sailboats for 2 people. **Optimists** are single sailed, solo crewed boats, particularly suitable for the younger helm. Why not pop along and get yourself or your children involved.

St Bridget's Church

There is no evidence as to how old St Bridget's Church actually is, it has been altered and extended many times over many centuries. It is known that Christians worshipped there at the time of the first Millennium, which gives an approximation of when it was first in use. The earliest parts of the building still surviving and visible are the Vestry Doorway and some of the masonry on the North wall of the Lady Chapel, which are of the early 14th century.

The church tower is mainly 16th century, although built around an earlier core the date of which is unknown. The church has a ring of 8 bells, 4 of them are over 200 years old. The bells are still in use and a skilled team ring for Sunday morning services as well as weddings and other special occasions.

Much of the East wall of the chancel and chapel is of 15th and 16th century construction dates, although the window tracery (the stone divisions within the window) is a Victorian renewal of old works. There was a major restoration of the church in 1869 / 1870 by the architects Kelly and Edwards of Chester. They rebuilt the aisle walls and replaced the arcades (the arches) which had been removed in the 18th century. At the same time, and in the years afterwards, a number of very fine fittings were added, including the stained glass and ironwork.

The church also contains the famous "Hogback" stone, which is of Anglo-Norse origin and dates from the early eleventh century from the Norse (or "Viking") settlement of Wirral's past. It represents evidence of Christian burial and the use of this site for Christian worship at the last Millennium.

The tracery of the East Window behind the High Altar is almost identical to that at Shifnal Church in Shropshire, but otherwise it is unique in design. The font which dates from the restoration of the Church, is based on a Norman design and is wide and deep, allowing in theory for baptism of children by total immersion (and for adults to sit in it and have the baptismal water poured over them). The Stained Glass is almost all to the design of Charles Kempe, thought by many to be the premier Victorian designer. It spans almost his whole career, from the Chapel east window of 1870 through to the dormer windows in the roof of 1906 / 7.

Inside the church there is a plaque to Johannes Van Zoelen who died while embarking with William of Orange's army which sailed from Hoylake to attach Ireland in 1689.

St Bridget (or Brigid, Bride) was a contemporary of St Patrick, born about the year 455, traditionally to a pagan father and a Christian mother. She founded a religious community at Kildare, and became Abbess. Religious communities in the Celtic Church were often centres of study and evangelism, and Bridget is thus one of those responsible for the spread of the Gospel in Ireland. God's grace in Bridget was remembered throughout the Celtic world, hence the dedication of this church.

The Parish of St Bridget's also houses the "Charles Dawson Brown Museum" which is in the old school building, adjacent to St Bridget's Church Centre, and contains exhibits showing the history of the fabric of St Bridget's Church over the last thousand years. In addition to Sundays, St Bridget's Church is open on Wednesday, Thursday and Friday afternoons from 2:00 to 4:00.

A church has stood on the site of St Bridget's for over 1000 years providing a focus for the West Kirby community. Across the churchyard lies the Community Centre incorporating the old school rooms built in 1825. Over the years the centre has continued to serve the Church and community.

The pyramidal roofed building was later added to house the Charles Dawson Brown Museum. In 1969 the centre was extended to provide more accommodation for the Church and community. Uses are varied and include Church and community groups of all ages. In addition the museum contains artefacts providing a history of life in West Kirby.

The current Church Centre lies within the attractive West Kirby Old Village Conservation Area including the Church, the Churchyard, the old school rooms, the Rectory and Rectory Field. The centre is housed in sound sandstone-faced old school rooms and a less attractive 1960s extension which is situated behind the old school rooms. The design and materials of the extension means that its life span is limited. The Church has been extensively renovated in the past and is now in good condition.

The Viking Hogback Stone

The "Hogback" stone is of Anglo-Norse origin, and dates from the early eleventh century and is of Norse origin. It represents evidence of Christian burial and Viking settlements across the Wirral Peninsula up to the 1st Millennia. Documentary evidence is limited, but it seems likely that the Norsemen arrived in Wirral (and elsewhere on the north-western seaboard) from Ireland in the tenth century. Their arrival was primarily for settlement rather than military occupation, and there seems to have been a gradual conversion to the Christian faith. Indeed, many of those arriving seem already to have been Christian, hence the dedication of the church to St Bridget, Abbess of Kildare. The Norse settlers have left their mark on this area not only in the "-by" ending of many place-names, but in the sculptural tradition of crosses and stones, including our own "Hogback" Stone. The stone was discovered during the restoration of St Bridget's Church in 1869-1870, traditionally having been unearthed on the site now covered by the aisle in which it stands.

It was originally preserved in the Charles Dawson Brown Museum adjacent to the former Schoolroom. Its recent transfer into the church is paralleled by the display of similar stones in other churches (e.g. Gosforth and Aspatria in Cumbria). There remain in the Museum a number of examples of Cross fragments from the same period as the stone, as well as artefacts of a later date. A visit to the Museum can be arranged by contacting the Custodian, Mr Rod Tann on 0151-625-1234 or the Rector on 0151-625-5229. The stone is carved from hard, grey, sandstone, not of the local variety. A similar stone is found in the district of Ruabon, near Wrexham North Wales, although some have argued for a Yorkshire origin. It is similar to other stones found in the north west of England, north Yorkshire, and southern Scotland. The popular generic description "Hogback" relates to the curving top of the stone, although the West Kirby example has been damaged in this area. However, the likely origin of this style is in imitation of Saxon stone shrines (e.g."Hedda's Tomb" in Peterborough Cathedral), which are themselves inspired by the gabled tombs of the Christian Mediterranean world.

The "Hogback" sculptors also imitated contemporary buildings, hence the curved roof, and often also curved sides, giving to some stones a "boat" shape. Many Hogback stones imitate a tiled roof, but on this example the tiles have become so stylised as to resemble large tear drops. The decoration on the side of the stone is a late example of an interlace or "plait" which can be found on much sculpture, Anglo-Norse and Celtic. The "cart-wheel" pattern found above the tiles is unusual, but is similar to designs on a cross on the Isle of Man. The quality of carving is not of the highest order, notice how the sculptor has failed to join up the interlace work. He has also carved against the "grain" of the stone, so that exposure to rain, frost and ice has caused the damage to the top portion. As well as the damage to the top of the stone, it seems that at some later stage in its history the ends of the stone have been lost, perhaps deliberately cut off, perhaps so that the stone could be used as a lintel or in a wall. All the surviving "Hogback" stones have been found within parish churchyards and scholarly opinion is that they served as markers for the burial place of important members of the Norse community, some stones perhaps being combined with head and foot stones, and even with standing Crosses.

Heritage walk

AN eight-mile Viking churches heritage walk will take place on Saturday, July 28.

The walk will start at St Bridget's Church, West Kirby, follow the banks of the Dee Estuary along the Wirral Way to Neston where it will end at St Mary and St Helen's Church.

Viking expert Steve Harding will show the famous Viking hogback tombstone at St Bridget's and at the end of the walk he will show the Neston cross fragments - believed to recount events in the life of a Viking couple holding hands and one of the fragments also records the earliest record of a jousting contest.

Steve said: "This will be an important precursor to next years big Viking "Olsok" walk/pilgrimage from St Bridget's through to St Olave's in Chester to commemorate the feast of St Olav which will become an annual international event."

For more information

about the walk and to register go to www.nottingham.ac.uk/~sczsteve/Olsok.htm

Walkers who would like to take part but require return transport from Neston to West Kirby should notify organisers by Thursday morning.

● Steve Harding with members of the Viking heritage group Wirhalh Skip Felag Code NA

West Kirby Convalescent Home

West Kirby Convalescent Home began in Filey Terrace by admitting six children so that they could benefit from good clean fresh air, good food, dedicated care and attention. The prevalence of children suffering from the effects of bad housing, neglect, debility and diseases such as tuberculosis, rheumatism, rheumatic fever, rickets, typhoid, bronchitis, in the 1880's it was recognised by the founders of the Home who provided the first accommodation in the Hoylake Cottage.

The present site was acquired and the hospital block was built in 1899, which was ultimately to benefit many thousands of children, by co-operation with the founders of a hospital. Children in the hospital block at the Convalescent Home, who were of longer stay than the majority of the other children, created pressure on the voluntary teaching which was first provided. Therefore, a certificated teacher was appointed as Head teacher and a school, recognised by the Board of Education as a Day School attached to a Home was opened in 1901.

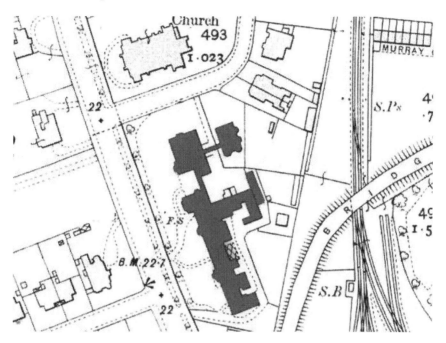

West Kirby Convalescent was the first school in the country to be recognised for the education of physically defective children. In 1905, the Board of Education recognised the school as a Boarding School. Moss's Directory for 1906 shows that the Matron was a Miss Agnes Giddins who was assisted by sixteen nursing staff. During 1918 the Home received children from London, Lincolnshire, Staffordshire, Worcestershire and Yorkshire, as well as from the local area. Various Education Acts had been passed which recognised the growing importance of Special Education. During the war, of the 3,424 children admitted, a high proportion of the medical cases were admitted under the Emergency Hospital Scheme. The discovery of Penicillin treatment by antibiotics and other factors resulted in the improvement of the general health of children. So there became less demand for places. The significance of change and the importance of education were recognised by the change of title of the establishment. The new title adopted in 1959 was the 'Children's Convalescent Home and School.

The 1960's brought great changes. The number of convalescent children continued to decline but the number of school children increased. The Department of Education raised the approved accommodation to 160 children and plans for further extensions to the school were made in 1970. The Warnock Report published in 1978 indicated that all children should be seen in terms of their individual needs, many would benefit from being transferred from special schools to mainstream schools, though there would always be the case of retention of some special schools. During this decade there was consolidation of the education services at West Kirby and with an ever-widening curriculum to children with a wide range of disabilities. Successful examination results were recorded and outdoor activities flourished. Much attention was paid to the preparation of school leavers in order that they would be fitted to meet the challenges of life after school. In 1979 the Childcare staff was then brought under the control of the Head teacher. Consequently the Term 'Home' was to be no longer used and was replaced by the present title of 'West Kirby Residential School'

West Kirby Ashton Park

The Park was first conceived by the Urban District Council of Hoylake and West Kirby when they announced their intention to build a large town park in West Kirby. Most of the land (9.8 acres) was leased from Miss Emma Mary Ashton, a wealthy spinster residing in Kensington in London who owned a sizable area of West Kirby land, land that was over the years to be developed for housing.

The other part (3.1 acres), at the Church Road end, was glebe-land and leased from the Church. Miss Ashton was the daughter of a Liverpool merchant called Ralph Ashton, who in turn was the son, and for a period, partner of Henry Ashton. Henry was a wealthy merchant but was born in Wigan into a family of linen manufacturers. The park was eventually started in 1900 and opened in 1901 when still only partially completed. The park continued to develop – tennis courts, bowling-greens, pavilions and shelters were provided, eventually a children's playground was built and a range of tennis courts provided in the Upper Park in the 1920's.

The look of the park has changed substantially over the years with the growth of the trees, remodelling and provision of additional sports and play facilities. The standard of care and maintenance has varied considerably over the years, sometimes to the detriment of the park. However The Park has enjoyed something of a revival since the creation of the Friends of Ashton Park in May 1991.

It is clear that the park was named after the Ashton family, most probably after Miss Emma Mary Ashton who leased most of the land making up the park to the Hoylake and West Kirby Urban District Council in 1899.

The original name was West Kirby Park. It is not known at the present time when the name was changed but on her death in 1935, aged 90 years; it still appeared to be called West Kirby Park. There was disappointed comment on her death in a local newspaper that the park was not left to the Council in her will. Nevertheless, at some stage it was to become Ashton Park.

Ashton Park, West Kirby

Hilbre Island

Hilbre Island

With thanks to the friends of Hilbre island who provided much of the information on the island.

Hilbre Island, West Kirby

Hilbre Island is one of a set of three islands in the Dee estuary off the coast of West Kirby. The three tidal islands, Little Eye, Middle Eye and Hilbre Island and the surrounding foreshore's, are the freehold and managed by Wirral Borough Council. Hilbre Island is approximately 47,000 square metres in area, and lies about 1.6 km from Red Rocks, the nearest part of the mainland of the Wirral Peninsula. The other two islands are called Middle Eye (or in older sources Middle Island), which is about 12,000 m² in size and Little Eye only 12,000 m². All three islands are formed of red Bunter sandstone. The Main Island and Middle Eye (See Below) are several hundred metres apart with Little Eye being nearly 1 mile away from the main island.

It is believed the that islands have been occupied on and off since the Stone Age with several finds of Stone and Bronze Age items and Roman pottery items were discovered in 1926. Although not named directly, it is believed that the islands are mentioned in Doomsday book. Mention is made of West Kirby having two churches, one in the town and one on an island in the sea. During Roman times we know that the island was inhabited and permanent residents were on the island of Hilbre as the island provided an important signalling and defensive outpost for Chester.

A small cell of Benedictine monks from St Werburgh now known as Chester Cathedral (See Above) became established on the islands some time before 1080 and the island became a common place for pilgrimage in the 13th and 14th century. Around this time a beacon of fire was established on the island to guide the mariners, the upkeep of which was paid annually at the sum of 10s. The last monk left the island in about 1550 as they were no longer considered a sanctuary as it had become a centre for commerce and a busy trading port, so much so that a customs house was established on the island to collect taxes on the goods traded.

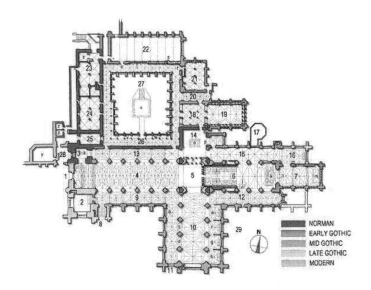

Above is a layout of the area of the church and which parts date to different eras and below is a depiction of Benedictine Monks.

S.BENEDICTVS   MAURUS

EXO FLI RECEPTA MGSTRI

It has been suggested by some local historians that a Saxon monastic cell already existed prior to the Conquest. The evidence for this essentially dates from the nineteenth century when a cross and grave cover were discovered, as well as a grave containing four skeletons, giving rise to a rumoured "Monks Graveyard"

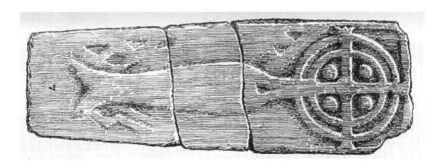

The grey sandstone grave-cover c1100 was found in 1864 in the place then believed to be the ancient cemetery on the island. Only the upper portion now remains and this is kept in the Charles Dawson Brown Museum near St. Bridget's Church, West Kirby

The carvings on the cross head however, have been dated to only around c1030, while the age of the skeletons has never been identified. While this suggests that an early monastic link with Hilbre is doubtful, there is enough evidence to suggest that it was perhaps a place of religious retreat and pilgrimage to a shrine of St Hildeburgh, many years before being colonised by monks after the Norman Conquest.

In 1692 a small factory was set up to refine rock salt. There was also a beer house or inn established on the island for the thirsty traders. There are tales of wrecking and smuggling taking place on Hilbre, and these ventures would certainly have taken place to some extent. Local gossip in the early 19th century also notes that the Hilbre innkeeper of an unconfirmed name was a very wealthy man who alleged to add to his income by robbing the dead bodies of unfortunates who drowned and were washed ashore by the tide onto the Island. However with the silting of the Dee, trade switched to the ports of the River Mersey and the trade vanished from the island leading to the closure of the beer-house. Part of the structure of this building remains incorporated in the Custodians Residence today. In 1841 a telegraph station was built on the island as part of a chain of signal stations which ran from Holyhead in Wales to Liverpool in England. They relayed weather conditions and other important information to and from ships at sea and the ports. The lifeboat station was erected shortly after in 1849 as an alternative deep water station for when Hoylake lifeboat was unable to launch at low tide.

Hilbre Boat

Today Little and Middle Eyes are both unpopulated, but Hilbre Island has a few houses, some of which are privately owned, and some where the Warden of the islands lives. The Islands are said to be named after St Hildeberg which is a corruption of a 17th century Mercian Saint Edburge and suggests a small religious house was on the island before the Norman Conquest. There is a small 3m high solar-powered lighthouse on the islands now operated by Trinity House. It was established in 1927 by the Mersey Docks & Harbour Board Authority, now the Mersey Docks and Harbour Company. The islands are tidal and can be reached on foot from the mainland at low tide. This is a popular activity with tourists, especially during the summer months. Until the end of the 1970s, there was a route from Red Rocks in Hoylake, but this has now been closed because of the danger of being caught by the tide and visitors are advised to set out from the town of West Kirby.

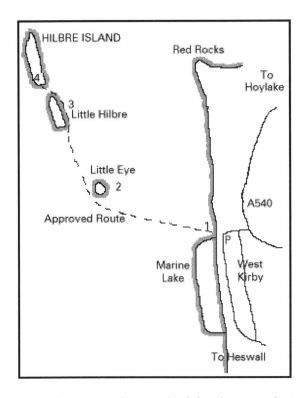

Little real archaeology remains on the island now, what relics have been found have been placed into care or into a museum. Finds include a sandstone cross head, a cross in a wall slab, a old masonry well, arrow head, Roman beads, port & sherry bottles, 17th century pottery and clay tobacco pipes. Probably the most interesting finds were in 1864 when human remains were unearthed and an 11th century grave slab; most likely part of the small graveyard suspected of being on the island. The foundations of several buildings from different periods still exist no doubt some related to the old salt works. When the Norman sepulchral cross was unearthed it was clear that it had been utilised from a later period by placing it in part of the end wall of the stable. On closer examination it had been white washed to protect it from the elements.

Recent excavations in 2007 revealed the remains of an unknown building floor with some walls and a door way but little else of value. On the West side of the island is a cave known as Lady's Cave where it is said that a body of a woman forcibly taken from island was washed up after drowning with her captors from being wrecked off the rocks. Other caves on Hilbre are reported to have been used for illicit purposes, the island having witnessed many wild scenes especially when the public house was in existence.

In 1819 William Daniel travelled around the coast of Britain and published a book of his journey. An extract reads:

"At the mouth of the Dee, off Cheshire shore, are three small islands, which it was our object to see. They are small scraps saved from the general waste committed on this coast by the sea, in consequence, i imagine, of being a little more elevated than the land by which they were surrounded; but they are gradually falling away, being all composed of sandstone, so soft that it may crumble

in your fingers. We landed on the larger more remote of them, called "Hilbre Island" which is almost half a mile in circumference and lies distant a little more than a mile from the mainland. Upon it there is a public house, the only habitation, and a few rabbits, the only quadrupeds, to which nature supplies a very meagre provision, only part of the island being covered with scanty sprinkling of grass. It is most important as a station for two beacons, which are raised upon it as guides to vessels through the swash, a channel between Hoyle Sands leading into Hoylake. An admirable road stead for ships of 600 tons burden. There is another entrance into this road; but the wind in any degree from the eastward, the swash is the only outlet by which vessels can escape".

William Webb in 1622 wrote:

"Here in the utmost western nook of this promontory, divided from the land, lies that little barren island called Ilbree or Hilbre, in which it was said there was sometimes a cell of monks, though i scarce believe it; for that kind of people loved warmer seats than this could ever be". 1

An extract from A Perambulation of the Hundred of Wirral by Harold Edgar Young in 1909 reads:

"I set of on my pilgrimage to spot where at one time rested the shrine of the lady of Hilbree, for it was here the Benedictines monks of Saint Werburghs established a small cell dedicated to the virgin Mary May back was now set fairly to Hoylake, and i went forward over the sands to visit the three islands, the largest and westernmost, Hilbre, then Middle Eye, whilst south of both i stood for a moment of Little Eye, just to say i had been there. They are called islands about twice a day, embraced by Neptune only at the

---

1 William Webb, 1622

full tydes and twice a day shakes hands with Brittayne. Although William Webb doubted the fact that there was a cell of monks on Hilbre, and very celebrated place it was, and miraculous too, for Richard Earl of Chester who when a young man, was performing a pilgrimage to St Winifreds Well in Flintshire, nearly opposite the islands, was set on by a band of Welsh marauders who drove him for refuge to the abbey of Basingwerk, where, not feeling too secure, by the advice of a monk of the cell of Hilbre, he addressed himself to St Werburgh, who is said to have instantly parted the waters of the Dee throwing up a huge sand bank, over which his constable, the Baron of Halton, marched his men to the rescue and that is why the sands are called the Constables Sands. Not the slightest traces of the cell remain, but a relic of the early church of Hilbre was found about 1853, consisting of a fine cross of red sandstone, said to be of the ninth or tenth century, similar in design to some still remaining in Ireland, and what appears to be a sepulchral cross is built into the wall of an outhouse, but it is covered with whitewash, as is the rest of the building, and its form is only revealed on a near examination. There is also a well, nearly 40 feet deep, cut through the solid rock, and which may possible have been sunk by the monks". 2

Mr Ferguson Irvine published a book in 1895 called Village Life in West Kirby 300 years ago, which reads:

"300 years ago a somewhat eccentric Lincolnshire knight, a certain Mr Richard Thimblebye, after whom Thimblebyes tower of Chester walls was named, was a resident on the island as a tenant of Sir Rowland Stanley of Hooton, though how Sir Rowland came to be the land lord i am at a loss to conceive. In addition to Sir Rowland there must have been several ship owners' living on the island of Hilbre, for in the list of shipping for 1572, mentioned

2 A Perambulation of the Hundred of Wirral. Harold Edgar Young, 1909

above, 11 of the ships are definitely stated to be of "Hilbre" and only 1 from West Kirby. And in 1544 six ships are entered at Chester as of Hilbre and 1 from Caldy. 3

Another account by Mr John Brassie of Tiverton of date unknown writes:

"About 40 years ago, being of child, I was one of the boys of the Chamber to Abbot Birkenshaw, then abbot of St Werburghsm Chester and by reason thereof familiarly acquainted with Dom John Smith or Dom Robert Harden, monks dwelling on the isle of Hilbree. I stayed for a fortnight together at certain times at which i had seen fish taken for the monks use within the water running about the island with nets, but whether with boat or not i doth not remember, and further saith i never heard that the said monks paid any tythe (tax) of fish taken there to the parson of West Kirby or any other, for the saith isle was then taken to be of no parish, but was called a cell, belonging to the monastery o Chester and therefore free from all manner of tythe paying". 4

Another witness states that he lived at Hilbre with the monks for 14 years, his account reads:

"I knoweth very well that the said prior monks had a fishing boat called Jack Rice and used to fish there by their servant, and I had often seen much fish taken their for their use. The monks had certain kine on the same island of Hilbree and yet paid no tithes of the same".

---

3 Ferguson Irvine, Village Life in West Kirby 300 years ago, 1895
4 John Brassie

The Lighthouse:

John Scott, the Earl of Chester, contributed ten shillings (equal to £369 in 2002) per year to the monks for the lamps of St. Mary between 1232 and 1237. However, it is not clear whether or not the lights were used for navigation in the River Dee. In 1813 Hilbre Island acted as a station for two beacons which guided vessels through the Swash, a channel between Hoylake sands to Hoylake on the northern coast of the Wirral.

Today, Hilbre Island Lighthouse, which is on Hilbre Island, off the north-west coast of the Wirral Peninsula, is a small automatic lighthouse and is a port landmark for the Hilbre swash in the River Dee. It came under the control of Trinity House in 1973 and before this was operated by the Mersey Docks and Harbour Board. Hilbre Island Lighthouse was converted from acetylene gas to solar powered operation in 1995.

Hilbre Island Wildlife:

Lying right in the mouth of the Dee Estuary Hilbre Island is in a prime spot for bird watching. There is something of interest every month of the year with the birds falling in to four broad categories – estuary birds, sea-birds, migrating land birds and breeding birds:

Estuary Birds

The most obvious group of birds to be seen from Hilbre for most of the year are the waders. Hundreds feed on the seaweed covered rocks around Hilbre at low tide with peak numbers during the winter. One to catch the eye is the Oystercatcher with its striking black and white plumage and bright red bill. Much rarer is the Purple Sandpiper, a Hilbre speciality with up to 50 wintering on the island. They can be hard to spot as they are well camouflaged foraging around the seaweed covered rocks. Waders also use the three Hilbre Islands as high tide roosts where they can rest, hopefully in peace, for a couple of hours. Both Little Eye and Middle Eye hold hundreds of Oystercatchers and Curlew. The roosts at West Kirby and Hoylake can be seen from the islands; here many thousands of Dunlin and Knot spend high tide. Other estuary birds include the Shelduck, a colourful duck which spends low tide feeding on the mud of the estuary and at high tide many can be seen swimming around Little Eye. Another Hilbre speciality is the Brent Goose and up to 50 overwinter on the islands. More often than not they can be observed on the rocks on the north end of the main island at low tide but at high tide they prefer either Little Eye or they fly further in to the estuary.

Sea birds

Hilbre is nationally famed as one of the best sites in the country to see Leach's Storm Petrel. This is a small ocean going bird which during its southward migration in Autumn can get blown in to the Irish Sea by westerly gales and end up off the mouth of the river Mersey where they battle against the wind to make it back out to sea by flying past Hilbre. Late summer sees a large post breeding gathering of Sandwich, Common and Little Terns. These graceful birds fill the air with their strident calls for several months before making their way south for the winter. Other regular sea birds are Gannets, Manx Shearwaters, Little Gulls, all four species of Skuas and a good selection of sea ducks, divers and grebes

Migrating Land Birds

Lying out to sea Hilbre Island acts as a magnet to any land bird flying along the coast or may be taking a short cut across Liverpool Bay. Virtually anything can turn up but some of the more regular visitors are Meadow Pipits, Willow Warblers, Swallows and Wheatears. Many birds which we don't normally think of as migrants can travel tens or even hundreds of miles during spring and autumn. Birds such as Robins, Blackbirds, Chaffinches, Green Finches and even tiny Goldcrests are seen flying in from the Irish Sea, many of these are trapped and ringed by members of the Hilbre Bird Observatory before being safely released.

Breeding Birds

The Hilbre Islands are largely free of ground predators and this means the population of breeding birds is denser in relative to the mainland. Typically about ten species breed on the islands with Shelduck, Meadow Pipits and Linnets being the most common, each with about 10 to 15 nests. Linnets are on the Red Data list so are of particular importance to Hilbre. Mallard, Skylark, Pied Wagtail, Wren, Robin and Carrion Crow also breed regularly.

The Hilbre Bird Observatory was established in 1957 to monitor all these birds. Whenever the Observatory is manned (typically 210 to 230 days a year) a full list of both the species seen and numbers is made. Many of the birds which pass through the islands are caught in the traps set by the Observatory members. The birds are measured, weighed and ringed before being released safely. The information gathered by the Observatory is used to study bird population trends and migration patterns; a Hilbre Bird Report is produced annually. Over the years a good number of rarities have been seen (and sometimes caught) by members of the Observatory. These include Little Shearwater, Surf Scoter, Laughing Gull, Gull-billed Tern, White-winged Black Tern, Bee-eater, Red-rumped Swallow, Red-throated Diver, Sub-alpine Warbler, Pallas's Warbler and Woodchat Shrike. For more details about the Hilbre Bird Observatory see their website (*www.hilbrebirdobs.co.uk*).5 The Dee Estuary Birding Website (*www.deeestuary.co.uk*) also

5 *www.hilbrebirdobs.co.uk*

covers Hilbre Island with daily bird news and a monthly newsletter.6

Hilbre has two sorts of wildlife communities: the estuary shores, and maritime heath with grassland. Rocky shores are usually rich in species, but here, the sandstone is crumbly, and so many shellfish (molluscs) cannot attach themselves. Estuarine sea water varies in its salt content at different times of tide, and after heavy rain water run-off from the land. Silt and sand are carried in the water, and moved around from the River Dee and Liverpool Bay. No living species is isolated; there is a complex inter-connection of animals and plants through their food, predation, ideal situation on the shore, etc. Disturbing the balance of one species can upset the whole pattern.

_____

6 *www.deeestuary.co.uk*

Effects of salinity and salt winds

Some animals are damaged by alterations in salt concentrations in sea water, but shore crabs can stand a range of salinity. Hilbre's prevailing winds come from the North West, their drying effect damaging to land plants and to shore animals when exposed between tides. The danger comes from winds drying out delicate living organisms as a windy day dries washing. Seaweeds and animals on the shore must shelter or have some protection when exposed by the falling tide. Mechanical wind damage wears away cliffs, its blown sand acting like blast-cleaning a building. This is evident where sandstone walls have worn away in the pattern of the masons' chisel marks. Salt chemically destroys land plants, and some are adapted to the drying effects by storing water in their leaves, such as purslane and scurvy grass. Sea thrift has the same internal protection against salty soil as other plants have to avoid frost damage. Air temperatures in winter are generally mild because of the effect of a large body of sea water which cools slowly. Snow is rare on Hilbre.

Shore invertebrate animals include red beadlet anemones, and worms in sand or stuck to the rocks. These have population cycles, peaking roughly every 20 years. Some shellfish (molluscs) live below the lowest tide levels in the sand and mud. Their shells and egg cases are often washed up, such as whelks and necklace shells. Dog whelks and winkles move over the rocks, feeding on algae, or each other! Mussels and barnacles sieve food from the sea water when covered by the tide. Sabellaria reef worms also filter sea water and build grey crusts on the western shores. Hermit crabs take over empty shells of dog whelks and common winkles. Edible crabs, once common, have almost died out. Shrimps and prawns inhabit pools in the sand.

Seaweeds show their usual shore zonation on Hilbre, with the exception of channelled wrack. On Hilbre, there is only one place where it is locally common, where the soft sandstone rock has a harder seam through it. Bladder wrack and serrated wrack are the least resistant to drying, and so found on the lower shore. Because there are no sub tidal rocks to anchor the plants, Hilbre has no Laminaria (oar weeds or kelps)

Sea vertebrate animals include Atlantic grey seals, occasional dolphins and porpoises, and whales. The Dee supports one of the few British non-breeding colonies of grey seals. Numbers have grown from a few animals in the 1930s to several hundred.

Fish species include gobies in the pools, flat fish (plaice, dab and flounder), in the gutters. Hilbre's only poisonous fish are weevers, which hide under the sand with their stinging spines exposed. Sea fish numbers have fallen in the last 100 years. It is difficult to know whether over-fishing has contributed.

Land mammals seem to be casual visitors to the islands. Foxes and hedgehogs have been seen walking over the shore, and weasel was recorded in the 1960s. Rabbits were introduced in the Middle Ages as food for the monks, but died out in the 19th century. Field voles live in the grassland.

Land plants include sea thrift, yellow birdsfoot trefoil, sea spurrey, buckshorn plantain, white sea campion, and centaury. Ragwort, poisonous to cattle, provides food for the striped caterpillars of cinnabar moth. These support many other butterflies, such as migrating painted ladies. Hilbre's specialities are the sea spleenwort, growing on sheltered cliff faces, and a sub species of rock sea lavender found in only a few other places in Europe. Small stone walls protect the plants from destruction by waves breaking over the island during storms. Bluebells are hybrids between the native and Spanish types.

Because of Hilbre's position in the River Dee estuary, where migrant birds feed every winter, it has been a special place to see wading birds and wildfowl (ducks and geese) for hundreds of years. The rocky shore also supports invertebrates such as several species of sea anemones, crabs, annelid worms, and molluscs such as winkles and mussels. In the past, the river was used as a salmon fishery. The grass and heath land vegetation of the islands supports nesting birds such as skylarks and meadow pipits. There was once a rabbit warren, kept as a source of winter food by the medieval monks, and mentioned in later leases.

Since the 1930s, a non-breeding colony of Atlantic Grey Seals has increased from about 10 animals to more than 500 at their peak in August. Many of them disappear in autumn to breed in west Wales, and possibly Scotland. Others remain here all year, hauling out at low tides on the sandbank to the west of Hilbre.

After World War II, Hilbre was bought by the local council, as a public open space, and a place to enjoy wild life. It has since been granted several titles and forms of protection, which are increasingly vital in a world where industrial development and over-fishing have destroyed many river and sea shore habitats. The Hilbre Bird Observatory was founded in 1957 by local experts, who continue to monitor the migration of many species of worldwide importance. Most of these are winter visitors, which migrate to the Arctic Circle or northern Europe to breed in the spring. In autumn they move south to warmer quarters in Africa. The Dee provides winter visitors with vital food in the form of invertebrates in the mud and sand of the shore. They rest on the rocks at high water, and it is important that they are not disturbed, as they waste energy every time they fly up. They live near to their energy limits, and a small amount of disturbance could mean that they starve to death.

In Britain, a system of Local Nature Reserves (LNRs) and Sites of Special Scientific Interest (SSSIs) was set up by successive

Governments from about 1960 onwards. Hilbre is an LNR, and part of the larger SSSI comprising the Dee Estuary and the Red Rock salt marsh. There is legal protection for the wild life here, and penalties for disturbing breeding species.

European recognition followed for the estuary, as a Special Protection Area {SPA}. The Dee Estuary is at present a candidate for EU Special Area of Conservation. In the 1990s, the Dee and Hilbre were together given further status as a protected wetland area under the international treaty signed at Ramsar in Iran in 1976. Ramsar sites in the many countries involved are those which shelter important populations of wetland species, especially birds. The original Convention issued a statement, accepted by all the governments concerned, that it provided "conservation and wise use of wetlands and their resources by national action" and by international agreement.

Hilbre Islands' owners, Wirral Metropolitan Borough Council, and national organisations such as English Nature and the RSPB continue to look after this precious site, while allowing the public to enjoy its beauty. Following the Country Code is a guide to sensitive tourism.

Dwellings on Hilbre Island

The islands have historically been used by fishermen and as a stop-off on the voyage from Chester to Ireland, as a result of which a public house had been established by the 18th century at the latest. They have a more dubious reputation for wrecking and smuggling and the innkeeper in the early 19th century was said to be unaccountably wealthy. The present buildings date from the mid-19th century when a telegraph signalling station was built on Hilbre Island. The only permanent resident now is the Dee Estuary Ranger.

Signal Station

The signal system was set up in 1826 by Trustees of the Liverpool Docks and a Lieutenant Barnard Watson was given the job of setting up a line of semaphore stations from Holyhead to Liverpool using semaphore signals with arms swinging on a mast. The line of signal stations has been mentioned on the BBC Television "Coast" series in which it was stated that the record for a message was 27 seconds.

This was to transmit a four digit code which corresponded to a phrase in the code book. At the outset the station was to be at Hoylake but in 1828 Lieutenant Watson obtained the site at Hilbre Island for the executors of Dr. Trevor, the late rector of West Kirby. The present building dates from improvements made in 1841. The station was retained for use with the electric telegraph system in 1861.

In 1836 part of the island was sub-let by the Trustees of Liverpool Docks to Trinity House. They maintained all the navigation buoys in the Dee Estuary, the Mersey and Liverpool Bay. This station was superseded in 1876 by a new one at Holyhead.

Hilbre Island & Wind Generated Power

In February 2005 a small wind turbine was installed on Hilbre Island with the intention of generating enough electricity for the Victorian complex of buildings and other installations on the island. The wind turbine is approximately 20ft high and the diameter across the blades is approximately 9ft. The cost to build the wind turbine was about £15,500 and funding for the project came from the Wirral Ranger Service {£2,000}, Local Agenda 21 scheme {£2,000}, Windscape Energy Centre {£3,000}, with the remainder from the Proudman Oceanographic Observatory. Wirral Borough Council paid for the foundations to be dug (approximately £400).

The wind turbine provides the power for Proudman Oceanographic Laboratory's scientific equipment that is sited on the tall mast on the island. This mast was erected in the 1960s and replaced an earlier one put up in 1912, it was originally used as a giant theodolite to measure the height of sandbanks in the Liverpool Bay but with the introduction of satellite surveying and depth sounding it became redundant.

In 2002 the mast was shortened by about 20ft, subsequently various installations have been set up on the mast by Proudman Oceanographic Laboratory. Their equipment includes: radar, a rain gauge, a wind speed gauge, a wind direction indicator, a temperature gauge, a humidity gauge, two types of light gauges, and a new very accurate wind speed and direction indicator.

Webcam and telemetry equipment installed at the top of the mast by Steve Cumberlidge for Proudman Oceanographic Laboratory provides valuable visual information of the surrounding area.

Trinity Cottage

The house was built around about 1850 for the buoy master, by his employers; Trinity House is correctly called Trinity Cottage. Its use as a holiday home by the Hilbre Island Club (a gentlemen's club based originally in Liverpool) gave it an alternative name, used by the present Hilbre families.

Its Wirral Council name is the Buoy Master's House, and it will become the Hilbre Island Centre when all the work is done. Raising funds is proving to be a huge task, and Wirral Borough Council's officers are helping the Friends of Hilbre to search for and send off applications, as well as processing their own. If you would like to get involved and help raise funds or be a volunteer, contact the Friends of Hilbre Island.

thefriendsofhilbre@hotmail.com

Future Work

The Friends of Hilbre are trying to get funds to Wirral Borough Council to pay for the slip way's reconstruction, using as much as possible of the original stone, scattered by the storms of the last 4 or 5 winters.

The slip will not be used for boats; this is a nature reserve, so resting shore birds will be left undisturbed, and the slip way will become a piece of historic landscape, and a place for visitors to walk and enjoy the view of the open sea.

Nothing will be visible to the general public for a while, but this does not mean that frantic activity is not going on behind the scenes. The whole point of this project is to look after a valuable nature reserve, with a fascinating history, and access for the public to enjoy this wonderful place. Eventually, there should be courses

78

for schools, colleges, local societies, and university research projects, housed in the collection of buildings, which is at present barred to visitors.

<u>Please remember that when visiting Hilbre Island, to leave it as you found it. It is a protected nature reserve and the volunteers work hard to keep it clean and available for exploration.</u>

With thanks again to friends of Hilbre Island for providing the information, I take no credit for their work.

Hoylake

Hoylake

Hoylake has gone by many names over the centuries and has for the vast majority of time been associated as a residence for Mainers and fisherman. The old township grew up around the small fishing village of Hoose which is now amalgamated into local villages. The name Hoylake was derived from Hoyle Lake, which was a channel of water between Hilbre Island and Dove Point. The mainland was protected by a wide sandbank known as Hoyle Bank and with a water depth of about 20 feet; it provided a safe anchorage for ships too large to sail up the Dee to Chester.

In order to help guide mariners up and down the channel and allowing safe access into the Hoylake anchorage, two lighthouses were constructed in the 1760s. The lower light was a wooden structure that could be moved according to differing tides and shifting sands to remain aligned to the upper lighthouse, which was a permanent brick building. Both of these structures were rebuilt a century later with much improved structures.

The upper lighthouse as seen above, which consisted of an octagonal brick tower, had a magnificent red light. The lights stopped on the 14th May 1886 and are now part of a private residence in Valentia Road.

The mainland of the Hoylake area was protected by a wide sandbank known as Hoyle Bank and with a water depth of about 20 feet; it provided a safe anchorage for ships too large to sail up the Dee to Chester. In order to help guide mariners up and down the channel and allowing safe access into the Hoylake anchorage it was decided that lighthouses were required. In 1764, 2 lighthouses were built at Hoyle Lake. One was wooden structure the Lower light 24feet / 8metres high, which stood at the high water mark, and could be moved to accommodate differing tides and shifting sands and the second one, the Upper light; was built of red brick in an octagonal shape. In 1776 the Hoylake Lighthouse had four floors to accommodate the two families that took care of the two lighthouses. Eventually the weak wooden structures of the lower lighthouse were demolished and it was later rebuilt in brick in 1833, and again in 1865. The lighthouse formed part of the foundations of the old "Winter Gardens" cinema which is now demolished next to the Lifeboat Station.

In 1866 a new Upper lighthouse approx 52 ft (15.85m) high with a diameter at the bottom of 25 ft 9 in. (7.82m) and a diameter at the top 16 ft (4.88m) was built on the same spot as the 1764 lighthouse. The light was last lit on 14 May 1886. After the upper lighthouse in Valentia Road fell into disuse, the lighthouse keeper's cottage became a private residence. In a report of 1795, land was bought for use as a garden next to the Upper lighthouse and, in 1837; more land was purchased in order to prevent property development which would conceal the lighthouses from the sea.

It is recorded that the Perch Rock and the Hoylake lighthouses would fly a Blue flag to summon the lifeboat if somebody was seen in distress. 1909 Captain Edward Cole Wheeler bought the Upper Hoylake Lighthouse for £800 (equal to £46,101.86 in 2001) and Charles Bertie Burrows bought the Lower Hoylake Lighthouse for £936 10s 00d (equal to £53,967.99 in 2001). The upper lighthouse, consisting of an octagonal brick tower, which had a magnificent red light still exists today however it has been overcome by modern housing and now occupies a private residence in Valentia Road. The lower lighthouse, which was the closest to the shore in Alderney Road, continued to work but was deactivated in 1908 and finally demolished in 1922. Many old photographs and postcard remain showing the lighthouses and thus these structures have become part of Hoylake's heritage.

The lower lighthouse, closer to the shore in Alderney Road continued but was deactivated in 1908 and finally demolished in 1922. Many old photographs and postcard remain showing the lighthouses and thus these structures have become part of Hoylake's heritage.

Modern Hoylake was once the two ancient villages of Little Meols and Roose, which until 1833 were in the parish of West Kirby. The coast of Little Meols stretched from Riverside Road in West Kirby to the bottom of Alderley Road where Hoose began. The present name of Hoylake is derived from the "High Lake" or "Heye-pol", which once extended several miles along the coast from Hilbre to Dove Point at Meols.

At low tide it had a depth of up to 20 feet of water and was protected by a wide sandbank, known as Hoyle Bank, providing a safe anchorage for ships that were too large to sail up the Dee to Chester.

In the 17th Century Hoylake was one of the main embarkation points for troops sailing to Ireland. Thousands of soldiers, civilians, infantry and cavalry sailed from Hoylake, including in 1690, King William III and his 10,000 men strong army. The soldiers "would often sally forth bent on wine, and were proficient in robbing a hen roost or rounding up a few ducks".

During the 1700s the River Dee became more difficult to navigate. Docks were built at Liverpool, and inbound ships waited at Hoylake for the tide and a suitable wind to sail up the Mersey. At the time, smuggling was prevalent in the Dee and Irish Sea. Several local men worked as "customs officers", aboard special yachts stopping and searching vessels. A more dangerous occupation was as a guide to incoming vessels through the sandbanks of Liverpool Bay. In 1770 three pilot boats were wrecked and 28 people drowned.

By the 1830's the silting of the lake could not be curbed and the cutting of a new channel to Liverpool, marked the end of Hoylake's shipping heyday.

Fishing now became the main trade for the local community and the clear waters of the Dee were teeming with fish. In the 1850s five fishing boats could catch 17 tons of fish in one night, but domestic conditions could be harsh. Cottages in Seaview and Lake Place were home to fishing families. Many had up to 10 children, living without modern conveniences such as sewers, drains, gas or electricity.

In contrast to the poor fisher folk, affluent people visited Hoylake. They were attracted to its splendid beaches and enjoyed the new "craze" of sea-bathing.

Hoylake developed as a holiday resort when Lord Stanley had The Royal Hotel built and the place became noted for the high social standing of its visitors. "Almost all of them are of the nobility and gentry", a contemporary correspondent reported, and for the genteel young Victorian lady seeking a pastime to fill the hours between breakfast and lunch, Hoylake provided a fascinating variety of sea shells and seaweed. The shells were made into souvenirs by being attached to pin cushions and engraved 'A Present from Hoylake' whilst the seaweed, or flowers of the sea as they were called, would be mounted in albums, a hobby favoured by Queen Victoria.

It was a welcome change for this part of The Wirral to be favoured by respectable people, as for many years it had an unsavoury reputation as being the haunt of smugglers and wreckers, with the inhabitants of the Public House on nearby Hilbre Island, alleged to add to their income by robbing the dead bodies of unfortunates who drowned and were washed ashore by the tide onto the Island.

In 1796 an advertisement for the Royal Hotel, in Stanley Road read. "A terrace has lately been added to the hotel, from which there is a fine view of the lake, the sea, the Lancashire hills and Welsh mountains and of every ship which goes to and comes from Parkgate and Liverpool".

From 1840, Hoylake had the added attraction of a racecourse which was laid out on a rabbit warren facing the Royal Hotel. The turf was reputed to be the finest in the world. Although it ceased to be used in 1876, the western turning is still visible, and two of the old railing posts still stand.

Golf firmly established the name of Hoylake nationally and internationally. The present Royal Liverpool Golf Club was originally a nine-hole course founded by local enthusiasts in 1869. Hoylake's sands of time shifted yet again with the coming of the railway in 1866. It transformed the sand-buried, shrimp-smelling village into a major seaside resort and commuter town.

Market Street

Market Street is the main road through Hoylake which since the creation of the town has played a huge role in its development. Market Street is essentially the high street which most of the commercial ventures have sprung up around. Once a road of small shanty huts and street vendors the road has now developed and contains many restaurants, public houses and a large variety of shops.

Tourism still plays an important part of Hoylake's economy and of an evening a variety of trendy wide bars and fine dining spring to life. Once a year during the August bank holiday the lifeboat station has an open day and the promenade at Hoylake becomes a bustling area packed with people watching air shows over the beach, playing at the fairs or simply visiting the local shops and stalls.

Hoylake is still a great place to visit if not for the relaxed clean promenade then for the sunset across the Dee which looks out across Hoylake's green fields and historic seaside town.

This old photo of Market Street seen above was taken from around the junction with Elm Grove and facing toward Meols. The "Hovis" buildings on the left are where the library is today. The buildings on the right therefore must be Hoylake School of Dance and the offices for accountants Ainley Cookson. That sandstone, protruding wall is the side of The 3 Sisters grocers.

The above photo is of how Market Street can be seen today.

SCOTCH HOUSE.

JOSEPH ILES,

FAMILY

Baker and Confectioner,

PLAIN AND FANCY BISCUIT BAKER,

36, MARKET STREET,

Branch: 102, Market Street,

HOYLAKE.

Our Milk Brown Bread is strongly recommended by the most eminent medical men.

Madeira, Plum, Sultana, Rice, Seed, Balmoral, Lemon, Sponge, and Luncheon Cakes. Chocolate Sandwiches. Birthday, Christening and Bride's Cakes made to order.

HOYLAKE Van deliveries daily. WEST KIRBY Van deliveries on Mondays, Wednesdays, and Saturdays.

Above is a picture of the original Punch Bowl on Market Street. The original building was demolished in the 1930's in order to widen the main road. Below is how it is seen today.

The Hoylake Lido

Hoylake's Lido was an outdoor swimming pool and was located on the promenade. It was opened in June 1913 and rebuilt in the late 1920s at the cost of £25,000. The use of the baths increased and for a short time the residents achieved notoriety.

In 1976 the Hoylake Pool and Community Trust took over the running of the facility from Wirral Borough Council. The baths finally closed in 1981 when many of the swimmers began using the facilities of the West Kirby Concourse. Many people still remember the pool and the activities that went hand in hand. Kay Morgan who was Women's Captain in 1931 can still recall the lido's time at the centre of the early years of the club's life, she commented:

"We used to wear woollen swimsuits but that was just all there was. There was no lycra. We went about 7 o'clock in the morning before we went to school. The temperature was about 50 degrees Fahrenheit (10 centigrade). There was usually quite a crowd of us and we were pretty tough".

Pinky Stabback competed in synchronised swimming at the club during the 1960's, she recalls:

"In the summer they used to have what they called Aqua ballets in all the outdoor pools that were still going strong in the 1960's. But then gradually it became more serious. To be a good synchronised swimmer these days you need the stamina of a middle distance

runner, the agility of a gymnast, the grace of a ballet dancer and a decent ear for music because you've got to have a good sense of rhythm and the heart of a lion because it is very very hard work."

Hoylake Amateur Swimming Club has recently put together an exhibition which includes photographs, memorabilia, and historic cinema footage of the pool, filmed in the 1930's and 40's. Give them a browse on your travels.

The Royal Hotel

The Royal Hotel was built by Sir John Stanley in 1792, with the intention of developing the area as a holiday resort. The numerous steam packet vessels sailing between Liverpool and North Wales which called at the hotel provided valuable patronage. Business boomed for the hotel and it soon gained reputation for being one luxury within the peninsula which at the time lacked in this type accommodation. In 1840 the Royal Hotel in Hoylake had the added attraction of a racecourse which was laid out on a rabbit warren facing the Hotel. The turf was reputed to be the finest in the world. Although the course ceased to be used in 1876, the western turning is still visible, and two of the old railing posts still stand. Like many of the old buildings in Wirral the Hotel fell into disrepair and unfortunately the hotel building was demolished in the 1950s.

An extract from Gentleman's Magazine dated June 1796 reads as follows:

"The hotel lately erected by Sir John Stanley lord of the manor, is situated within a few yards of the beach, and contains a variety of commodious apartments, both public and private, very comfortably furnished. The charges are very moderate, the table well and amply supplied, and nothing is wanting on the part of the persons

who have the management of it to render this house as pleasant and convenient as can be desired"7

In 1796 an advertisement for the Royal Hotel, in Stanley Road read:

"A terrace has lately been added to the hotel, from which there is a fine view of the lake, the sea, the Lancashire hills and Welsh mountains and of every ship which goes to and comes from Parkgate and Liverpool".

Hoylake's well known swimming pool known as "The Lido" was located on the main promenade. It was opened in June 1913 and rebuilt again in the late 1920s at a large sum to the borough. In 1976, the Hoylake Pool and Community Trust took over the

---

7 Gentleman's Magazine June, 1796

running of the facility from Wirral Borough Council. The baths finally closed in 1981.

Many people from the Hoylake area still remember the spectacular baths were many local competitions were held and the general public could go for a great time or simply to relax.

Hoylake maritime history has taken a huge fall due mainly to the silting up of the river Dee. At one time Hoylake was primarily full of fisherman and maritime related trades, indeed it is most probable that Hoylake was founded on this principal. With the silting of the river, inevitably came the slowing of commerce and the larger vessels were unable to navigate the shallow treacherous waters. Most vessels now moved to Liverpool or the river Mersey on the other side of the peninsula. There is much recorded evidence of the gradual silting of the Dee which caused great trouble not only to Hoylake but all of the villages which spring along the Dee coastline.

An extract from A Perambulation of the Hundred of Wirral by Harold Edgar Young in 1909 reads:

"Even fifty years ago there was a fair depth of water in the Hoyle Lake, and the steam packets used to take passengers, mostly visitors to Hoylake, for day trips to various places on the opposite coast of North Wales, the fishermen charging sixpence each for putting passengers on board the packets. Today Hoylake, for all practical purposes, has ceased to exist, and the large fishing boats now dock at Liverpool. However Hoylake has another attraction, and their splendid golf links are counted amongst the best in the kingdom, but her sea trade is a thing of the past and is not likely to be recaptured. Now Hoylake is a place of residence for those who collect their income elsewhere, and the old sand blown road, with the links on one side and wide hungry looking fields on the other, that used to connect Hoylake with West Kirby is called a "drive"

and large and pretty houses cluster along it all the way to West Kirby. Pedestrians now leave that road to motorists and cyclists preferring to take their way with hesitating footsteps, and a pang of conscience across the golf links for to be sure they will spoil some mans drive and add their knowledge of Agot".8

Like its neighbour West Kirby, the promenade once famed for its magnificence during the Victorian era has slowly declined and now with only intermittent maintenance the promenade is slowing fading in oblivion. Much of the area was given a revamp prior to the 2006 Open held at Hoylake however the area still needs a large sum of money investing in it in order to bring the town back to its former glory. The beach at Hoylake still sees its fair share of visitors but it is no comparison to the crowds that used to flock to the beaches during the summer in the early 20th century.

---

8 Harold Edgar Young, A Perambulation of the Hundred of Wirral, 1909

The Promenade, Hoylake

Hoylake Community Centre

The Centre is situated in Hoyle Road, Hoylake and was originally built as a Higher Elementary School in 1909 and opened for educational purposes in January 1910. The site is next to the seafront road, North Parade, which in later years provided the school its better known name- 'The Parade School'. Some 80 years later in 1988, the school was closed and the buildings began to deteriorate. Whilst the main building was used for some years to house the local authority's 'Hoylake Youth Club', low usage of the premises induced the authority to put it up for sale for redevelopment as private housing. However, the impending loss of yet another Hoylake amenity united the townsfolk to fight to preserve the building for the community.

In 1992, a Steering Committee was formed and its members set out to establish the Centre as a focus for community life and activity in the local area. It also created a constitution and formulated a Joint Management agreement for the centre (the first in Wirral). In February 1993, at Wallasey Town Hall, a formal Joint Management agreement was signed on behalf of the JMC and the local authority granting the JMC a 25 year lease on the buildings. The agreement enables the committee to manage the Centre on a day-to-day basis. During that year charitable status was also obtained.

The premises have now been transformed into a thriving, bustling Community Centre. A dedicated team of volunteers (including members of the original Steering Committee) run the Centre. With vision backed up with hard work, the centre has turned from an abandoned derelict school to the valuable, all-purpose Centre that the local and wider community enjoy today.

Hoylake Lifeboat Station & Museum

Hoylake and West Kirby are situated on the north west corner of the Wirral Peninsular overlooking the picturesque Dee Estuary, with the hills of North Wales as a backdrop, as attractive as the scene is the famous Sands of Dee are also notoriously treacherous, with many a vessel having come to grief on the various sandbanks and many a modern day visitor being caught out by the speed of the incoming tide.

The inshore Lifeboat Station West Kirby was established in 1966, together with a similar station at Flint on the opposite side of the estuary to cope with the growing number of incidents in the area, The Hoylake Lifeboat station dates back to 1803 and celebrated its Bi-Centenary in 2003.

Hoylake Lifeboat station is one of the oldest on the coasts of Great Britain and Ireland, and was founded by the Mersey docks and Harbour Board in 1803 and taken over by the RNLI in 1894. For a time there was also a Lifeboat Station on Hilbre Island in the Dee Estuary which was also manned by the men of Hoylake, this Station was closed in the 1930's.

Another photo of the old lifeboat station, featuring a chap named H Cummins of West Kirby with his donkeys and trap was taken circa 1912.

And whilst we are mentioning donkeys, I must mention this photo below showing the old donkey and carriage service that took people over to Hilbre Island. The old lifeboat station can be seen in the background alongside the long-gone lower lighthouse.

Hoylake

Hoylake has always had a "carriage launched" lifeboat. At first the boat was pulled to the water by a team of horses, frames for storing the harnesses can still be seen on the wall in the current boathouse which was built in1899. Today the lifeboat and carriage are towed by a caterpillar tracked Talus tractor which has been specifically designed to launch carriage lifeboats.

Since the RNLI took over the station, two silver and five bronze medals have been awarded to the crewmen of Hoylake.

On 22nd of December 1810, the Hoylake Lifeboat was tasked to a vessel called "Traveller", she was aground in the River Mersey in a fierce storm and in danger of being lost, on her way to the casualty, The Lifeboat was swamped by an enormous wave and eight of her crew perished.

In 1902 a Silver medal was awarded to Coxswain Thomas Dodd for the rescue of the crew of nine of the Barque Matador of Riga, on 16 and 17 October in a severe gale and very heavy seas, The Imperial Russian Association for Life-Saving on Waters awarded the crew their First Class Certificate of Merit for this service and this illuminating certificate is still on display in the boathouse.

In 1943 Bronze medals were awarded to Coxswain Herbert Jones, Lifeboat man Ben Armitage and Coastguard WJ Widdup for the rescue of the occupants of a small dingy that was out of control on lee shore, in a strong westerly wind and very rough sea.

The coxswain considered the time it would take to muster the crew, launch and position the Lifeboat would take too long, so a rowing boat was used to rescue the casualties.

A Bronze medal was awarded to Coxswain Harold (Danny) Triggs for a service to the tug "Diane" in which two lives were saved, the tug had sunk and the men were on the wheelhouse roof when Coxswain Triggs put the Lifeboat alongside and plucked the men to safety.

In 1979 a bronze medal was awarded to Coxswain Harry Jones and the RNLI thanks on Vellum accorded to Second Cox, John McDermott and crewman David Dodd (both men later Coxswain) for a service on 20th September when the lifeboat saved the catamaran Truganini and her crew of three in a westerly storm and very rough seas. Medal service certificate were awarded to other crewmembers, Geoff Ormrod (later Coxswain), Peter Jones, Alan Tolley and Gordon Bird.

In August 1992 the present lifeboat Lady of Hilbre was involved in the rescue of a Polish yacht and her crew of nine during the Tall Ships Race. In very rough seas and a full gale the yacht was eventually towed to safety in Birkenhead. Coxswain John McDermott and all his crew were congratulated by the RNLI for fine seamanship and professionalism.

A new future for the Victorian Lifeboat Station

For a number of years, local enthusiasts had been searching for a possible site for a Hoylake Lifeboat Museum. Already the Museum collection was coming together. At its heart was the historic lifeboat *Chapman*. Built at the end of Queen Victoria's reign, *Chapman* is the oldest surviving Liverpool-class lifeboat and also the last to be stationed on Wirral's Hilbre Island. She had been saved from dereliction by Bill and John Parr and was ready for display.

The relocation of the RNLI in Hoylake provided the perfect opportunity. A campaign led by Hoylake man John Parr as seen below, captured considerable local support and a local benefactor stepped in to buy the buildings to lease to the enthusiasts group. On 3rd March 2011 Hoylake Lifeboat Museum Trust was formed and that summer the Museum opened to the public for the first time.

The RNLI are always looking for help and donations, they hold annual festivals on the August Bank Holiday which is always a great event, so pop along for the day and show your support.

With thanks to the RNLI for providing the information and history of the iconic Lifeboat station.

The Royal Liverpool Golf Club, Hoylake

Built in 1869, on what was then the racecourse of the Liverpool Hunt Club, Hoylake is the oldest of all the English seaside courses with the exception of Westward Ho in Devon. Robert Chambers and George Morris were commissioned to lay out the original Hoylake course, which was extended to 18 holes in 1871. The course received the "Royal" designation in 1871 due to the patronage of the Duke of Connaught of the day, who was one of Queen Victoria's younger sons. For the first seven years of its life the land still performed its original function, doubling as a golf course and a horse racing track, indeed, echoes of this heritage can be found today in the names of the first and eighteenth holes, Course and Stand, while the original saddling bell still hangs in the club house. Once the horses had been dispatched to pastures new Hoylake began to take its place in the history of golf in general and of the amateur game in particular.

The course is a prestigious one and liked by many professional across the world, the events taken place here speak for them self:

The Open Championship:

1897, 1902, 1907, 1913, 1924, 1930, 1936, 1947, 1956, 1967, 2006

Walker Cup:

1983

Curtis Cup:

1992

The Amateur Championship:

1885 (the inaugural event), 1887, 1890, 1894, 1898, 1902, 1906, 1910, 1921, 1927, 1933, 1939, 1953, 1962, 1969, 1975, 1995, 2000

Ladies' British Amateur Championship:

1896, 1989, 1996

The Ricoh Women's British Open is one of the golfing highlights of the sporting calendar. In its 37th year, this year's Championship makes its first appearance at one of the most famous and historic links courses in the UK, Royal Liverpool Golf Club at Hoylake. The seaside club has been host to 11 Open Championships is a fitting stage on which to perform for the world's leading players over what will be 4 memorable days from the 13th – 16th of September, 2012, a new date ensuring the tournament does not clash with the London Olympics.

A bit of history also known locally is that a young John Lennon used to walk across the course to visit his girlfriend and future wife Cynthia Powell who lived in Hoylake.

Meols

Meols

Although called Melas in the Doomsday Book, the name Meols is from the Old Norse word for sand-dunes. Meols was once an ancient seaport. Up until a century ago it was called Meolse but the name was changed when the railway station was built -- the story has it that the railway managers were unsure of the spelling and had assumed it to be the same as Meols, near Southport. In Victorian times, Meols was still a farming community although a few houses were built by the gentry. It was only a small village and didn't have a school or church and the villagers had to walk to the parish church at Hoylake where the children attended the Hoylake National School.

The population of Meols was 140 in 1801 but, with the arrival of the Birkenhead Road in about 1850, it had increased to 821 in 1901. The first inn in Meols was the Sloop Inn. It dates back to at least 1840. John Cookson was understood to be the first landlord in occupation in 1841. It later became a shop and was demolished in 1938.

"The Old Sloop", Meols.

The original Railway Inn was pulled down in the 1930's when it became fashionable to build larger inns to attract the motorist. The new inn was opened on 1st December 1938 and then the old one was knocked down to become the car park. St. John the Baptist Church was consecrated on 12th April 1913, the foundation stone having been laid on 21st October 1911. The first Anglican services in the 1880's were held in the schoolroom.

In June 1901 a temporary church was opened at a cost of 500 UK Pounds this was later to become the church hall. Between Meols and Moreton / Leasowe is a submerged forest. Roots and stumps of large trees are partially buried in peaty soil, which is the result of a pre-historic forest becoming submerged by the sea encroaching on the land. Although the remains of this forest had not been seen for several decades, they were visible in the spring of 1982.

In 1846 the Revd Abraham Hume was visiting the parsonage in Hoylake, Wirral. He noticed some ancient artefacts, including a Roman brooch on the mantelpiece. Hume asked how they got there and learnt that local fishermen had found them on the shore at Meols. Realising the importance of the finds, he made efforts to recover further objects.

Meols, on the north Wirral coast, is now seen as one of the most significant ancient sites in the north west of England. For thousands of years, people had made use of a natural harbour called the Hoyle Lake. This gave its name in modern times to Hoylake, the town which grew up nearby. During the early 19th century storms and high tides had progressively washed away occupation deposits from a succession of settlements along the north Wirral coast. In less than a hundred years the shore-line retreated nearly 500 metres at Dove Point. Metal items from these layers were deposited on the beach where they were later found. The objects range from the Neolithic through to the 18th century. There is a strong emphasis on the later medieval period but also a remarkable group of Roman, Saxon and Viking artefacts. After Hume began to publicise the finds in the 1840s, the site came to the attention of antiquarians who competed for the 'produce of the Cheshire shore'. Many amassed considerable collections. It is estimated that over a fifty-year period well over 5000 objects were found.

Selections of the finest were published by Revd Hume in 1863 in his remarkable book, 'Ancient Meols'. Over 3000 objects, including some illustrated by Hume, still survive in modern museum collections, spread between no fewer than six institutions.

Meols' importance through the ages was due to its coastal location beside the Hoyle Lake, a haven on the Irish Sea coast. The objects show that the port began to develop about 2400 years ago, during the Iron Age. Finds such as a silver tetradrachm (a coin) of Tigranes II of Armenia, minted in Syria in the 1st century BC and bronze coins of Augustus, suggest that there had been contacts with France and even the Mediterranean before the Roman occupation of Britain. It is probable that a major item of the trade was salt from the brine springs of southern Cheshire. Reassessment of the Roman finds suggests military activity at Meols in the pre-

Flavian period before the foundation of the fortress at Chester and perhaps a market function afterwards.

During the Roman period, the port grew to be the largest settlement in Merseyside. Over 70 Roman brooches and 120 coins have been found. This shows that Meols was a busy trading community. Ships sailing up the west coast of Britain would have stopped off to pick up goods or raw materials and trade pottery and other items. The local people may have lived in circular wooden houses, as the remains of such houses were found on the shore in the late 19th century.

Sloop Cottage

Home Farm

The Submerged Forest of Meols

The submerged forest of Meols is one of Wirral's strangest phenomena's. The prehistoric forest at one time stretched far out into what is now the Irish Sea consisting of a dense canopy of foliage inhabited by many breeds of animals lost since extinct .

Through natural tidal activities the water overran the forest and settlement and left the land which we see today at Meols. Here at low water the last remains of tree stumps and roots sunk into clay can sometimes be seen.

The first written record of the submerged forest was in the Iter-Lancastrense of 1636:

"But greater wonder calls me hence, ye deepe Low spongie mosses yet rememberence keepe Of Noahs flood, on numbers infinite Of fir trees swaines doe in their cesses lightAnd in summe places, when the sea doth bate Down from ye shoare, tis wonder to relate How many thousands of theis trees now stand Black broken on their rootes, which once drie land Did cover, whence turfs Neptune yields to showe He did not always to theis borders flow."9

Philip Sulley writes in 1889:

"The trees appear to have been thicker towards the Dee end of the Wirral with them becoming smaller and less dense towards Leasowe. The trees are mainly Oak, with some Fir, and appear to a certain extent, to have been planted. Many are of great size, in 1857 a tree 35 feet long was found. Some of the roots and trunks to be seen at low tide are of great thickness, and large quantities of wood have been taken from here, the black oak having been put to practical muse for making furniture. The inroads of the sea are so great that portions of the forest are being constantly washed away and a fresh surface laid bare inland. William banks who was resident here and discovered antiquities for more than half a

9 Iter-Lancastrense, 1636

century, states that the forest, as described by Dr Hume in his book on Ancient t Meols in 1863, has been completely destroyed. Yet there is no diminution in the extent, and doubtless this forest called submarine but more properly subterranean, extends for a considerable distance inland. It crops up at the banks of the Wallasey pool along the line of the new railway from Birkenhead Park to the old dock station; and was uncovered by the Great Meols railway station when the large ponds were excavated there".
10

More than just a forest

Of course the area did not just consist of a prehistoric forest. The finds have shown that a large settlement has existed here some distance from today's shoreline. The movement of the waters in this area is extremely heavy as can be seen with the disappearance of the lost church and the lost lighthouse at Leasowe, and we can conclude that this settlement was completely lost under the waters. In the latter part of the 19th century all that remained of the ancient

10 Philip Sulley, 1889

township of Meols were the foundations of mediaeval buildings, apparently of timber and plaster on brick, puddled with the blue clay precisely as at Hilbre.

The most interesting description is that of E.W Cox in 1895 which states that:

"The remains of circular stone huts, up to two feet below high-water mark, made of wattled wood coated with clay, and the ground was abundantly marked with hoofs of horses with round shoes, and with the foot marks of cattle, pigs and sheep".11

On the earliest reliable map which is that of Visscher in 1650, Meols is the only place in Wirral to have been recorded as having two separate roads leading in and out of it showing the growth of the community in that area. We can only wonder what archaeological treasure may lay beneath the water at Meols and Leasowe, but some local historians have already begun to try and find out. Peter France and John Emmett have teamed up with archaeological divers McDonald's Marine and American Sub Sea specialists' Deep trek. Together they are investigating the remains of a settlement at Meols and hope to show the results in a forthcoming television show on Discovery and National Geographic Channels.

The following is a report by Historian & Archaeologist David Griffiths of Oxford University on the remarkable collection of objects found in the sands by antiquaries in the 19th century:

The name Meols may not be familiar to many people, but the archaeological remains uncovered at this site on the north coast of the Wirral peninsula may be some of the most important evidence

---

11 E.W Cox, 1895

in Britain for prehistoric, Roman and medieval coastal settlement and trade. Meols was once the most important ancient port in the North-West. Then it eroded into the Irish Sea. During the 19th century, over 3,000 objects dating to between the Mesolithic and post-medieval periods were collected from the eroding shoreline. Some of the Iron Age, Roman and medieval objects indicate trade as far afield as Ireland, Europe, Scandinavia and the Mediterranean, and are exceptional as a regional group. But the finds also shed light on the everyday life of a remote community on the edge of the Irish Sea.

The name Meols (pronounced 'Mells') comes from the Viking word for sand banks or sand dunes, which dominate this landscape and tidal seascape. When standing on the concrete sea-wall looking out towards the Irish Sea, there is little obviously to suggest that this non-dramatic low-lying coastline was once the site of the most important port in the North-West.

From the end of the 18th century, there were major changes in the offshore channels and sand banks, partly caused by the beginnings of large-scale dredging on the approaches to the growing port of Liverpool. One of the effects of this was a sudden acceleration in coastal erosion at Meols. Throughout the 19th century, until the sea defences were completed in the mid-1890s, the Wirral coastline retreated southwards for up to half a kilometre in places. As large areas of dune sand were washed away by storms, extensive traces of ancient settlements along the coast were exposed. When the tide is out, the sands stretch offshore almost as far as the eye can see. One clue that this tidal zone was once dry land can be found on the beach from time to time. Patches of blackened mud with fibrous decayed wood are occasionally visible in the shifting sands. These are the last remnants of the forest which stood in late Mesolithic times in this area. Maps of the coastline in the 18th century show a low sandy promontory, known as Dove Point (the name comes from Celtic meaning black), which once existed to the north of the present coastline. As the dune sand was washed away during the 19th century, centuries of accumulated soil under the sand, together with middens and occupation deposits associated with later prehistoric, Roman and medieval settlements became mixed with the forest remains beneath.

From around 1810, people from the local villages of Great Meols and Hoylake began to find small metal brooches, mounts, pins, tokens, seals, pilgrim badges, coins and knives, glass beads, pieces of leather and worked wood, iron weapons, knives and keys, sherds of pottery and flint tools, all as far as they could see from within the remains of the 'Ancient Forest'. The finds created a stir of interest in the isolated fishing community. Some of the Roman brooches were used as toys by local children, and other objects were kept as curiosities. A boy described as 'deaf and dumb' was one of the more prolific collectors. More people went down to the beach to search, and word got wider afield. A Mr PB Ainslie of Liverpool had amassed a collection as early as 1817, but the first person to realise the archaeological significance of this material was the Rev Abraham Hume, a respected Liverpool antiquary. Hume noticed a group of objects owned by Mrs Longueville, wife of the Vicar of Hoylake, on display in the parsonage early in 1846. In July 1846, he read a short paper on the discoveries to an archaeological congress in York, and interest amongst other antiquaries grew.

Hume began paying regular visits to the Wirral shore to search the eroding layers himself. He encouraged local people to look for objects, and paid them a few pence for their trouble. He was soon joined by Henry Ecroyd Smith, the first curator of Liverpool Museum. In the 1860s and 1870s, Charles Potter also began amassing a collection, as did Edward Cox, an American merchant settled in Liverpool, Albert Way and J Romilly Allen. In addition, the wealthy Liverpool businessman Joseph Mayer purchased objects from the site to add to his varied collection of antiquities. Hume's monograph 'Ancient Meols', published in 1863, contained an illustrated account of the site, but interest in Meols continued until the end of the century. Much discussion, with yearly reports of discoveries, was published by Ecroyd Smith and Potter in the Transactions of the Historical Society of Lancashire and Cheshire.

Rival antiquaries

There was some personal rivalry amongst the antiquaries, and their collections, like those of the locals, were their own private possessions. Ecroyd Smith was the first to donate his discoveries and purchases to a museum, principally to the early holdings of Liverpool Museum, but in 1858 he also sent a small parcel of 'representative objects' to the British Museum (where it lay almost forgotten until it was rediscovered deep in the museum archive last year). Potter donated his collection to the Grosvenor Museum, Chester, where it remains the largest of the groups of Meols objects. Mayer's collection was, like Ecroyd Smith's, donated to Liverpool Museum.

But what happened to the other collections, and in particular, Hume's? There is some evidence that Potter may have purchased some of Hume's objects, explaining the unusual variety and richness of his donation to Chester Museum. Other pieces probably never found their way into museums. As the owners died, some after moving to other parts of the country, the objects may have ended up almost anywhere, including sadly in the dustbin. Smaller groups of objects from Meols (otherwise termed 'The Cheshire Shore', 'Hoylake' or 'Leasowe' after the neighbouring villages) have been identified in museums in Warrington, Birkenhead and even Verulamium. It is still possible that further objects from the site are lying forgotten in museum archives or private homes.

The 19th century finds were supplemented during the 20th century by a smaller but equally interesting series of chance discoveries, most recently by people armed with metal detectors searching on the beach. These finds are broadly consistent in type and date with the previous ones, and show that traces of the ancient site may still remain amongst the sands.

What do the finds tell us?

The presence of small groups of coastal hunter-gatherer settlers is suggested by the presence of Mesolithic, Neolithic and early Bronze Age flints, together with a tiny amount of Neolithic and Bronze Age pottery. The lithic finds, many of which are arrow heads, date back to the days of the forest, before the low-lying coastal lands were cleared and cultivated.

It is from the later Iron Age that long-distance trading connections seem to grow. Three coins of pre-Roman Carthage, together with two coins of the Coriosolites, an Iron Age tribe in Brittany, and a gold British coin were found. Perhaps equally interesting, very early Roman material of the mid-1st century AD - possibly from before the Roman Conquest - is also present. Claudian coins, a military belt-buckle and two Aucissa-type brooches confirm Meols as one of the earliest sites in the region producing Roman finds. In fact the Roman material, including glass and pottery, continues through to the end of the Roman Empire in Britain. Over 70 brooches and 120 coins point to a metalwork-rich, coin-using oasis in an economically undeveloped landscape. Indeed, Meols seems to have continued to trade with the classical world in the post-Roman period when few other sites in Britain were doing so. A pottery flask from the Early Christian shrine of St Menas, in Egypt, was found buried in mud on the shore in the 1950s, and more recently three 6th and 7th century Byzantine coins have turned up.

The Saxons and Vikings gave Meols a fresh lease of life as a port, especially after the Wirral was densely settled by Scandinavians in the 10th century AD. Hiberno-Norse ringed pins and a small bronze bell, strap ends, mounts, coins and over 20 Anglo-Saxon silver pennies are evidence that the site participated in a trading network which extended to Dublin, York and Scandinavia during the early medieval period.

Medieval wealth

These finds are, however, small in number compared to the hundreds dating from the 12th-16th centuries, which are the majority of those held in museum collections. The extent and range of the medieval finds from Meols is greater than those known from any site outside London, including towns such as York, Bristol and Salisbury. This is astonishing for an otherwise obscure coastal landing place. As well as objects of bronze, iron and silver, the fragile metal known as lead tin, similar to pewter, has also survived at Meols, adding hundreds of artefacts - mostly items of personal ornament such as buckles, pilgrim badges and brooches - which may have decayed to nothing elsewhere. The pilgrim badges include examples from Rome, southern France and several from Canterbury, but it seems that much else was being made locally. Some of the 14th century writing seals and later medieval cloth seals are apparently north-western products, indeed one is inscribed to Meols itself. An unfinished lead buckle suggests some metalworking was taking place at the site, and there are also crucibles. The medieval pottery and iron tools speak more of hard work and modest prosperity than of exotic trade links. It seems that as the medieval period wore on, Meols became less of a trading port and more of an ordinary everyday settlement. The presence of nearly two hundred medieval coins, however, reminds us that it must still have had a special role as a market site.

The Meols finds were almost all unstratified. Their immediate context was not recorded, and in many cases must have been destroyed by erosion before they were retrieved. Given the tendency towards rivalry of some of the antiquaries, could they have added objects from elsewhere, perhaps bought on the antiquities market, in order to impress their fellow-collectors? Could they have 'faked it'? The likelihood of this is not as great as it seems. The principal collectors were all very familiar with the sorts of material coming from the site, and could easily have spotted anything but a very clever substitution. Many of the Meols finds show evidence of exposure to sea water and the bronzes have a distinctive dark patina.

Recent research has also shown that almost all of the finds have some sort of regional parallel - they are mostly the sort of things which occur in ones or twos elsewhere in the North West, but not in these huge quantities. In order to have obtained the right objects from elsewhere to supplement their collections, the antiquaries would have had to have an extraordinary insight into the archaeology of the region. Moreover, many of the regional parallels which support the authenticity of the Meols finds were not found until the 20th century. For a place which produced this remarkable amount of material evidence, we have surprisingly little topographical information about the site. Maps and charts show the retreat of the coastline, and the gradual disappearance of Dove Point where much of the archaeology must have been located. The antiquaries, however, seem to have focused almost exclusively on collecting artefacts, as they left little by way of descriptions of any structures and layers. Hume seemed content to understand the strata present within the sand dunes. He was aware that there were archaeologically-interesting layers above the 'Ancient Forest', but he did not make any detailed record. Ecroyd Smith and Potter made some more tantalising observations. Ecroyd Smith referred to a 'British burial mound' and cremations. Potter described house structures in the eroding sand - round houses of wattle, beneath rectangular buildings with stone wall footings. These were surrounded by fences, middens and trackways. All of these observations sound convincing as descriptions of Iron Age, Romano-British and medieval domestic structures of types since excavated at other sites.

Viking burial

A recently re-identified group of iron weapons in the antiquarian collections, including a sword, a deliberately-bent spear head, an axe and a shield boss, suggest the presence of at least one pagan Viking grave at Meols. This could possibly link with some of the descriptions of burials. Exasperatingly for modern archaeologists, Ecroyd Smith and Potter did not record the detailed location of the burials and structures. There are, however, some clues in the dates of the observations, many of which were made in the 1880s and early 1890s. Ordnance Survey maps of this time show that the coast had already retreated considerably since the mid-19th century, and was not far off the present coastline, which was stabilised by sea walls shortly afterwards. If so, this suggests that the houses and graves cannot have been far out from the present shore. It also points to the exciting possibility that deep down in the sand behind the present sea wall, more of the ancient settlement may be preserved. What, then, was Meols? Was it a coastal beach market, a port, a group of villages, or even a forgotten town? It almost certainly had elements of all of these at different times. But we have very little documentary record of what happened there, and as far as we can tell, none at all before the name Meols is first recorded as a minor settlement in the Doomsday Book. There are no known documents of the kind associated with medieval ports and towns.

Yet the artefacts tell a story of settlement and trade over thousands of years, with peaks in the Roman, Viking and medieval periods.

The site is located at a point between two major river systems, the Mersey and Dee, with open access to the Irish Sea. Meols was also near several important territorial boundaries throughout history - Cornovian and Brigantian in the Iron Age, Anglo-Saxon and Viking, and English and Welsh in later times. Seasonal fairs probably supplemented the permanent presence. Lead from the Welsh hills may have been traded at Meols, possibly as long ago as the Iron Age. Wool, grain and Cheshire salt were exchanged there over many centuries. Perhaps the key to understanding Meols can never be found by studying one type of object, structure or period. Taking a step back from the detail reveals a geographically marginal place which went through numerous changes of fortune, but retained a special and unusual role as a trading centre over nearly two millennia.12

David Griffiths lectures in archaeology at Oxford University's Department for Continuing Education. He is working on the publication of Meols, together with Robert Philpott of Liverpool Museum and Geoff Egan of the Museum of London

David Griffiths, *British Archaeology magazine (December 2001).*

---

12 David Griffiths, *British Archaeology magazine (December 2001).*

Hoylake Cottage Hospital

The prevalence of children suffering from the effects of bad housing, neglect, debility and diseases such as tuberculosis, rheumatism, rheumatic fever, rickets, typhoid, bronchitis, in the 1880's it was recognised by the founders of the Home who provided the first accommodation in the Hoylake Cottage. The present site was acquired and the hospital block was built in 1899, which was ultimately to benefit many thousands of children, by co-operation with the founders of a hospital. Children in the hospital block at the Convalescent Home, who were of longer stay than the majority of the other children, created pressure on the voluntary teaching which was first provided. Therefore, a certificated teacher was appointed as Head teacher and a school, recognised by the Board of Education as a Day School attached to a Home was opened in 1901.

This was the first school in the country to be recognised for the education of physically defective children. In 1905, the Board of Education recognised the school as a Boarding School. During 1918 the Home received children from London, Lincolnshire, Staffordshire, Worcestershire and Yorkshire, as well as from the local area. Various Education Acts had been passed which recognised the growing importance of Special Education. During the war, of the 3,424 children admitted, a high proportion of the medical cases were admitted under the Emergency Hospital Scheme. The discovery of Penicillin treatment by antibiotics and other factors resulted in the improvement of the general health of children. So there became less demand for places. The significance of change and the importance of education were recognised by the change of title of the establishment. The new title adopted in 1959 was the "Children's Convalescent Home and School".

The 60's brought great changes. The number of convalescent children continued to decline but the number of school children increased. The Department of Education raised the approved accommodation to 160 children and plans for further extensions to the school were made in 1970. The Warnock Report published in 1978 indicated that all children should be seen in terms of their individual needs, many would benefit from being transferred from special schools to mainstream schools, though there would always be the case of retention of some special schools. During this decade there was consolidation of the education services at West Kirby and with an ever-widening curriculum to children with a wide range of disabilities. Successful examination results were recorded and outdoor activities flourished. Much attention was paid to the preparation of school leavers in order that they would be fitted to meet the challenges of life after school. In 1979 the Childcare staff was brought under the control of the Head teacher. Consequently the Term 'Home' was to be no longer used and was replaced by the present title of 'West Kirby Residential School'

In recent years Trustees at Hoylake Cottage have decided that day care facilities for older people should be provided in a purpose-designed, new building. After several months of deliberation including consultation with local residents, staff and service users, the charitable trust board decided that refurbishing the existing old building was not a viable option.

"This has been a very difficult decision for us as we have heard strong views from members of Hoylake Civic Society and several other local people who would like to keep this old building for heritage and nostalgia reasons," said Mr Taylor the Trust Board Chairman.

A survey was carried out during the summer to gather the views of the local community on how to redevelop the day care centre. A total of 100 forms were returned, of which 17 asked for the frontage of Hoylake Cottage to be retained. No one currently using Hoylake Cottage asked for the old building to be preserved. Respondents were asked which features would be most important in designing a new centre and most put open spaces with lots of natural light at the top of the list.

Mr Taylor said: "We have seriously considered the possibility of keeping the front façade of Hoylake Cottage and building new rooms behind it, because some people feel very strongly that they don't want to lose the look of the building. But our architects and other professional advisors tell us we would need a large contingency budget for all the structural problems which you only discover once dismantling work gets underway. It has become clear that we would be paying more for an inferior building if we tried to retain part of it, and that seems almost immoral. In the end, the decision came down to identifying what matters most and that has to be the people who use Hoylake Cottage."With a brand new design our architects will be able to give us ideas for creating the best possible environment for care where staff can continue to do the excellent work for which they are renowned."

And so the old building was demolished for creation of a contemporary building. In homage to the long history of Hoylake Cottage, the shape of the building drawn up by the architects retained the circular driveway and roundabout, setting back the new building in a similar position to the existing one.

In 2010, former Liverpool Manager Rafa Benitez and his wife, Montse, have donated an undisclosed amount to a Wirral charity.

Wirral Globe 10:07am Friday 25th June 2010

The couple gave the cash to Hoylake Cottage Hospital as Montse gives up her role as chair of the social events committee. She has helped to drum up support for £1.5 million appeal for a new day care centre for older people.

Mrs Benitez said: "I was very close to my granny who had dementia for ten years until she died. She had a nurse at home, but not everyone is so lucky which is why I wanted to help Hoylake Cottage.

"I will keep in touch with all the progress and hopefully once the new centre is built, I will come back to join in the celebrations."

Hoylake Cottage Chair of Trustees, Tony Twemlow, said the money will go towards the building of the new centre.

He said: "The gift from Montse and Rafa is extremely generous and we are all more grateful than we can say for their tremendous kindness. "Their donation will go a long way to helping us to build a centre which will provide relief to older people and those who care for them at home.

"Also, I would like to say a huge thank you to Montse for her support over the years. She has been a fabulous ambassador for Hoylake Cottage and has helped us to gain much needed support for our events and campaigns. I wish her and Rafa lots of success in their new life in Italy." A recent dinner also held by the pair was attended by LFC players raised £40,000 for the Cottage.

The Day Care Appeal will fund a new kitchen and laundry and a centre providing day care for older people and those with dementia, giving relief to those who care for them in their own homes. Work is expected to start later this year on the first phase of the plan, demolishing part of the old building in order to build a new kitchen and laundry.13

Meols Drive

13 Wirral Globe, Friday 25th June, 2010

Meols Drive is located within the North West corner of the Wirral Peninsula between the two urban centres' of Hoylake and West Kirby. Both are old settlements which grew as commuter towns during the later 19th and early 20th century, serving the commercial centres of Liverpool and Birkenhead.

The main development in the area consisted of large villas backing onto the Golf Course with slightly smaller detached, semi-detached or terraced houses on the Eastern side of Meols Drive towards the Hoylake Station. The present Golf Club House opened in 1894. The Golf Club is thought to be the second oldest in England.

Meols Drive and the golf course are linked both historically and physically. The one constructed to take advantage both of the other and the surrounding landscape and seascape. The golf course and the surrounding housing on Meols Drive, Stanley Road and Lingdale Roads provide the setting for the each other and are mutually dependent.

The Viking Boat of Meols

Archaeologists have discovered what they believe to be the first Viking ship ever discovered in Britain, buried beneath the Railway Inn car park at Meols. The vessel is thought to be a 1,000-year-old relic from the Norse occupation of the Wirral peninsular and was detected using state-of-the-art ground radar technology.

At 30ft long by 5ft wide, it would have been able to transport dozens of Viking warriors, as well as their goods and cattle. The boat has lain untouched and almost unknown since 1938, when builders employed by the Railway Inn in Meols stumbled across a fragment whilst laying the car park. Frightened that the discovery could hold up work, the foreman ordered it reburied, but not before one of the builders drew a quick sketch.

The drawing ended up in the hands of his son, John McRae, who handed it in to the local museum and authorities in 1991 after seeing a regional television programme about Vikings on the Wirral. There it lay, virtually unread, for more than a decade.

More links to our Viking past

MORE Vikings have been found in Wirral

By LORNA HUGHES

Scientists found two men from Meols shared identical historical links to Scandinavia during DNA testing.

Bizarrely one - Stan Royden - is married to a Norwegian woman, Mette, and is chairman of the committee for the Scandinavian Church in Liverpool.

The second - Roy Shuttleworth - is secretary of the Friends of Meols Park and has been looking into the area's Viking past.

Although not related, the men were found to have very similar chromosome types.

Their strongest DNA link was to Gotland, an island off the east coast of Sweden.

The findings were released this week and are the result of a DNA ancestry event held last November as part of the Nordic Festival in Liverpool.

Viking expert Professor Steve Harding from Nottingham University and colleagues Professor Mark Jobling and Dr Turi King at Leicester University tested 100 men free of charge.

A genetic survey carried out last year by scientists from Nottingham and Leicester Universities and University College London found that up to 50% of the DNA of men from old Wirral families was Norse in origin.

Mr Royden, 64, said: "I was quite surprised because I thought I was all Anglo-Saxon.

"I've always felt an affinity with the place - my first job was in Norway, which is where I met my wife Mette."

In another bizarre coincidence, the Scandinavian Church Stan is involved with is in the Diocese of Gotland and comes under the jury isdiction of the Bishop of Gotland.

Mr Shuttleworth, 56, said he was "totally amazed" by the results.

He said: "I couldn't believe it , especially as we're working on a Viking project in Meols."

Only men can be tested for the Viking link because the test is based on DNA from the male Y chromosome which is passed down the paternal line from generation to generation, with little or no change.

Professor Harding said: "The results for Stan and Roy showed the match in both cases was Gotland in Sweden, where 15% of men have the same Y chromosome type as Stan and Roy.

"They also have matches elsewhere around Scandinavia.

"We can't say for sure but there is a very good chance they are both carrying the Y-chromosome of a Viking. Don't forget the Vikings moved all a lot, so they didn't necessarily come from just one place.

"They're just ordinary men but in every cell they have this link to Scandinavia."

●A research paper on the Wirral genetic survey was published last year. Find out more at http://www.nottingham.ac.uk/~enzstev .

Professor Harding is giving a talk on Viking Wirral and Viking genes at Wallasey Central Library between 2.30 and 4pm on Mon, Oct 12.

For more information call 638 2304.

● Roy Shuttleworth (left) and Stan Royden (right) with Prof Stephen Harding.

Professor Stephen Harding of the University of Nottingham, who carried out the ground scans, commented:

"That was that until a few years ago when the pub made an application to build a patio. Then it was unearthed that the patio foundations were not allowed to go below a certain point, because of the boat. The pub landlord mentions this news to a few local people, including a policeman with an interest in Viking history, who told me".

Prof Harding, an expert on the Merseyside Vikings, paid £450 for a Ground Penetrating Radar (GPR) survey of the site, which revealed the precise location and dimensions of the vessel. He believes it is either a Viking transport boat, similar to a long ship, or a ship from the centuries that immediately followed the Viking era. It has overlapping planks, typical of Viking "clinker" boats.

"If indeed Viking, this would be a very major find anywhere in the world, and unique for Britain. If it is not, it is still very interesting." He is now applying for European funding to excavate the site, which would cost hundreds of thousands of pounds. The boat is thought to lie 6ft to 10ft (2m to 3m) underground. Any dig would probably be led by Norway's Dr Knut Paasche, the world's leading expert on Viking ships.

"You would have thought that it's an archaeologist's dream to have a major find in front of a pub entrance, but it's actually a bit of a nightmare. The dig would take months, and we would need the permission of the brewery and the pub," he said.14

Whilst Viking boat burial sites have been uncovered in the UK before, the wooden vessels have always been rotted away, leaving only their more durable contents. But the Wirral boat is preserved in waterlogged blue clay, and thought to be almost completely intact. Prof Harding says it could eventually be removed and displayed in a museum, or even made accessible from the pub's cellar, allowing patrons to enjoy a stunning historical view with their beer. The curious thing is that the Meols long ship is several miles from the coast; Prof Harding suggests that it could have been washed inland during flooding before sinking into a marsh.

---

14 Prof Stephen Harding

The Railway Inn

This pub should technically now be called The New Railway Inn, because it stands on the site of a former inn of the same name as seen above. The original inn could not be demolished until the new pub was built, because at the time the license had to be transferred from one premises to the other without a break in trading. The 'new' Railway Inn seen below opened along Birkenhead Road on 1 December 1938, allowing the old inn to be pulled down and the site turned into a car park.

The Roman Road of Meols to Chester

Through much effort, field work and research by local volunteers and archaeologists; it has been confirmed that a direct route did exist from Roman Chester (Deva) through to Meols. The road is thought to have been around 6 metres wide which was about twenty Roman feet, and was thought to be constructed from separate distinct layers of cobbles on a layer of larger stones.

The following information was written by local archaeologists Peter France & John Emmett.

The only dating evidence found within the road was pottery dating from the later first century to the early fourth century. The road was traced by K Jermy and others, based along the line of Street Hey Lane, East of Williston, appears to be aligned on the crossing of Wallasey Pool, close to the Penny Bridge. Further investigations by local archaeologist Peter France and John Emmett have suggested that this route, with some post Roman distortion forms the basis of the late medieval Blake Street.

The Roman line has been traced to point along the Noctorum Ridge. The Roman road has been found to diverge from the Meols road at a point in South Wirral at an angle of about 35 degrees, but the alignment projected back towards Chester points to the Northgate. Construction of this route is narrower than the other, at about four metres; and the layers are even thinner. The conclusion drawn from the study of these two roads is inescapably that the Birkenhead road is later than or sub-servant to, the Meols road. It is tempting to believe that the Hoyle Lake was used in naval campaigns in 60-80ad as a supply base especially as military occupation of Chester is now known to have predated the Agricola water pipe of 78ad.

Other routes are subject to ongoing investigations, especially those which were found to underlie the foundations of Birkenhead priory during the main restoration work of the late 19th century. This can be traced for some distance, taking in the famous Birkenhead ridge on the way.

There are two possible routes for this road in the Claughton / Bidston area but the general intention seems to have been to join the Chester to Meols route at a point just South of the latter. Watkins Roman Cheshire mentions a road leaving Chester to head out towards Blacon point and then run into Wirral parallel to the coast in a typically elevated position.

The magnificent survival of a length of this road runs through the former deer park at Shotwick, where its survival is undoubtedly due to lack of agriculture activities for centuries. It has been found to underlie the park enclosure bank and therefore must predate it. A section of this route was once marked on OS maps as a Roman road. Its true date, course and destination are currently under investigation, as it is felt unlikely that all North / South roads in Wirral were in use at any one time.

There was certainly a network of lanes and cracks linking farmsteads and other sites to the main lines of communication.

These are now nearly impossible to detect archaeologically. Many lengths of lanes or roads have traditions of being Roman in date but these are very difficult to verify, especially as no obvious alignment or construction details are known. An obvious example is the length of road discovered during the construction of the Manchester ship canal. This was stated to be made of stone and was buried beneath 15 feet of soil. It was aligned from the river bank to a point somewhere in the vicinity of Parkgate. Given the discovery of Roman practice earthworks not far away, and that the depth of overburden was identical to that which covered the Birkenhead bridge, this feature becomes worthy of further study.

It should be noted that the recent research into tide levels shows that the MHW level during the Roman period was about 15 feet lower than the present day level, and this makes the information more acceptable. It is unsafe to project any information out of hand without thorough investigation, especially when current thinking may dismiss it. Roman road construction was broadly similar right across the empire over hundreds of years, although the materials used would vary depending on what was available locally. The main ridge, or agger, was formed from material from the two lateral ditches. This gives the road its distinctive profile which we can recognise today on many sections. First, a broad ditch, the fossa, was dug. The base of the fossa was levelled and tamped down to form the pavimentum. A foundation layer called the statument, consisting of layers of flat stones embedded in earth or clay, was laid on top of the pavimentum. This provided a firm foundation for the road as well as allowing drainage. On top of the statument was a layer of sand or gravel called the rudus. This gave the road its resilience. A top layer of gravel, the nucleus, formed the road's surface. This may have been bound with concrete, but not necessarily. In towns, the surface may have been paved, but that would not have been the case in the roads around Ribchester.

Richard Mortimer of Cambridgeshire Archaeology has pointed out that the construction method described above applied to the Roman military roads, but there had been very successful and long-lived Iron Age societies before the Romans arrived, and these societies had roads and tracks of their own, many of which became 'Roman' roads. Even with the military roads, if there was no need to create the foundation they often wouldn't - a road over a good, hard gravel terrace would often only be de-turfed and ditched

The Roman roads were constructed from layers of stone, topped with hard-packed sand and gravel, which may have been bound with concrete. We can often see the remains of this metal ling today. In cross-section, a Roman road takes the form of a ridge, with a ditch either side. This ridge, or agger, often survives today, and is one of the most distinctive features of a Roman road. One or both ditches may survive, sometimes forming a convenient route for a stream. Where a road had to cross a river, a ford would have been easier to construct than a bridge, and we can see the remains of fords in rivers and streams. In order to ease the gradient when climbing a hill, or to level the road if it ran along the side of a hill, the Romans engineered cuttings and terraces. The "Line". As everybody knows, the Romans built their roads in straight lines. Often, when there is no other evidence, a straight line drawn between two confirmed sections of Roman road will indicate the course of the road.15

The Legend of Portus Setantiorum

The following is an article written by local historians John Emmett & Peter France, on the subject of the lost Roman port of Portus Setantiorum possibly being at Meols:

---

15 Peter France & John Emmett

The lost port of Portus Setantiorum is known to have been located between Anglesey and Morecombe bay. It is recorded on the maps of Ptolemy and others but the name is written in the area representing the sea in such a way that the precise location is difficult to determine. The map of Britain discovered by Charles Bertram under the parsonage of William Stukeley in 1755 actually shows the name pointing clearly at the tip of the Wirral peninsula. Although this map was denounced as a fake by some historians, some of the names of the Roman sites, unknown then, have subsequently been found to be correct and it would be unwise to disregard it today.

In their place names of Roman Britain, Rivett and Smith suggest that the name was first recorded by Agricola's fleet during a survey of the coats prior to a campaign in the North in 79/80 AD. This was recorded by Tacitus who also tells us that the fleet was employed to supply and support the land forces. If Agricola's base was Chester, this fleet must have been based at Meols.

The port was traditionally though to have been located at Fleetwood and this article will examine the case for both for and against this location. We will also put forward the suggestion that the port was located at Meols and we are well aware that no firm archaeological evidence exists at present to prove this case in favour of either site.

Fleetwood

The port of Fleetwood is situated at the tip of the narrow peninsula with the estuary of the River Wyre forming its eastern side. This small river's flows northward into Morecombe bay. There is a Roman fort at Kirkham a few miles to the south and a road is known to have left this fort in the direction of Fleetwood and to have led to the coast.

Roman finds have been generally few, the main ones being two coin hordes. Watkin in his Roman Lancashire mentions a square stone platform being discovered here, possibly the platform for a beacon. There is no list of finds from the shore comparable to Meols. It would appear that the main reasons for placing the port at Fleetwood are:

1. The position interpreted from the Ptolemy map
2. The Setantii, a sub tribe of Brigantes are known to have occupied the area
3. The River Wyre would provide a sheltered harbour for vessels

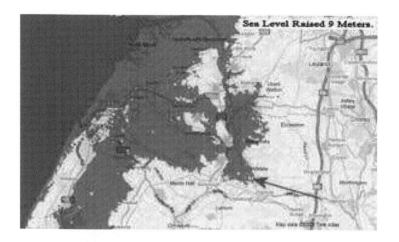

Examining these points it is acknowledged that there are many errors of longitude and latitude in Ptolemy and that he shows us that what is now Scotland somewhat skewed to the North East which will make a positive identification of the area unsafe. Indeed Rivett and Smith will not specify a location other than somewhere on the North West coast of England.

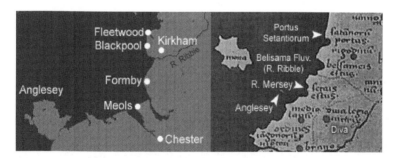

The Setantii have traditionally been though to occupy a relatively small area in Northern Lancashire and the port is supposed to be under their control, as the name implies. Recent archaeological research in South Lancashire has produced evidence that their territory did, in fact, extend to the Mersey, which was known as Setia. The Roman name for Lancashire at the time of writing is thought to be Galacum. Perhaps the function of the site at

151

Fleetwood was a small port with a signal station to give early warning to the naval force at Lancashire.

Meols

We must now turn to the site of Meols. It is clear that the large assemble of finds from the coastal erosion of the area indicates the prolonged use of this place over an extended period of time. The reasons for this are not difficult to understand. Meols was the largest Roman settlement on Merseyside. It pre-dated the more famous Roman outpost of Chester and was vital for supporting the land forces as they swept through England. That there was a Roman port at the top of the Wirral is in no doubt, but knowing its name is a different matter.

The effect of tidal range in the Roman period, as outlined in the Waddelove paper, helps us to understand the form and function of the coast, of North Wirral during that period. Here we can imagine the low promontory of Dove Point on the East with the island of

Hilbre to the West. Between these two points lay the deep and sheltered water of what was later known as the Hoyle Lake. This was protected to the seaward by Hoyle Bank and must have had the appearance of a lake. It is therefore easily understood why such a natural asset should be used almost continually over a long period of time. Despite being overwhelmed by the sea and sand during the mediaeval period, it was still considered to be fit for purpose by King William of Orange, and in the mid 19th century it provided a depth of five fathoms even at low tide.

We are now certain that this side connected to Chester by a direct major road during the Roman period. The lowest surface of this road has produced evidence contemporary with the foundation of the legionary fortress, which suggests that the military established themselves at the existing port almost on arrival to the area. We would suggest that it was at Meols that Agricola based his supply fleet for his campaigns in the North as this port was close in proximity to his headquarters, and communications need to be reliant on the wind and tide. The Dee has never favoured Chester as a port for larger vessels and difficult navigation up the constantly changing channels is well documented.

We have now suggested that Meols was a site of great significance to the Romans. Perhaps it was from here that Agricola looked out to sea and planned his conquest of Ireland, as described by Tacitus. He had intended Chester to be the capital of the Provence (Mason), which would be an ideal situation if Ireland had been absorbed in the empire. The rock channel was the main entrance to the Mersey, the present channel being improved in 1830, since when the rock channel has been allowed to silt up. We would suggest that this was the case in the Roman period that the Setia flowed out to the sea at Dove Point. It is therefore suggested that the main focus of activity was along the promontory, with the Setia on one side and the Hoyle Lake on the other.16

Conclusion

Having considered previous theories and added some of our own, we are now of the opinion, that the site of Portus Setantiorum lay at the Wirral port of Meols. There are known Roman naval bases at Holyhead and Lancaster, and Meols lies between them. It is also close to the legionary fortress and is the most important and practical natural harbour on this section of the British Coast. We are well aware of the lack of archaeological evidence at either site, but excavations at Meols may just possibly rectify this situation. It is the only major port noted by Agricola's survey.

The following is an extract from the Liverpool Museum in relation to Norse and Roman Settlement on the Wirral:

In the early medieval period Meols continued as a port, though now people traded with Ireland and the Mediterranean. Finds include a pottery flask, which contained holy water from the shrine of St Menas in Egypt and Byzantine coins from Turkey, dating from the 6th century AD. Later finds show that Viking settlers used the port too. In 902 AD the Norwegian Vikings were expelled from Dublin. Norse settlers, led by their chief, Hingamund, who left Dublin for England. Aethelfleda, Lady of the Mercians of Chester, granted them land in north Wirral. Viking place-names in Wirral show where they settled. The place-name Meols is derived from a Norse word 'melr' meaning 'sand dune'. Meols became a beach market where Viking traders could land their boats and exchange goods with other merchants. Viking ring-headed cloak

16 Peter France & John Emmett

pins from Ireland would be typical of the objects that were traded. A discovery came from examining the ironwork. Dr David Griffiths of Oxford University has recognised for the first time the contents of a Viking warrior burial, with a shield boss, spear and axe. This provided further evidence of the strong Norse presence in north Wirral.

The port of Meols was used right through the Middle Ages. Just as important, though, was the little farming settlement of Meols. About 1500 AD the villagers lost the battle against the sand dunes which finally covered the village. They moved a short distance to the south and established the new village of Meols where it stands to this day. Particularly important is the collection of later medieval objects. This includes a wide range of ordinary domestic items such as buckles and belt fittings, pottery, knives and agricultural implements. There are also personal seals, pilgrim badges and armour. Dr Geoff Egan of the Museum of London has described the medieval metalwork is the second most important group in the country after London.

Knives, spoons and pottery jugs give a glimpse of life in a medieval house. Clothes fittings, like buckles and belt attachments, and leather shoes would be the everyday wear of people. This necklace and brooch illustrated on this page though would have been of special importance to the owners. The discovery of a scale balance and a large number of coins is evidence of trade. Several stirrups show us that the villagers had horses while iron arrowheads would have been used for hunting. Evidence of farming comes from the iron tools that have been found, such as sickles for harvesting crops, shears for clipping wool and iron spades for digging the ground.

During the 19th century erosion helped uncover the foundations of a number of medieval houses. The houses, with their clay floors, had been hidden under the sand for many years. Visitors to the ruins mentioned seeing the footprints of cows and people on the old village street. Unfortunately, nobody recorded these finds in detail.

Parts of a late medieval (early 15th century) pewter necklace with leaf pendants. A rare survival of a base-metal version (for a man or woman of ordinary means) of the fashion for gold or silver collars worn by the aristocracy. It is likely that little survives of ancient Meols today. The coastal erosion which revealed the objects also destroyed the settlements. The objects collected by antiquarians in the 19th century and kept public museums form almost the only surviving evidence of what was once one of the region's most important ports. National Museums Liverpool has a small collection of material from Meols, from the collections of Joseph Mayer and Henry Ecroyd Smith. Unfortunately many objects were lost in the fire at Liverpool Museum of 1941. Other groups of objects are in the Grosvenor Museum, Chester, Warrington Museum, the British Museum, and the Williamson Art Gallery and Museum in Birkenhead.

Since 2000 a team of specialists from National Museums Liverpool, Oxford University, Chester Archaeology, the Museum of London and other institutions has been working on a major catalogue of the 'Meols' material, co-ordinated through National Museums Liverpool. The project aims to re-examine both the existing material and the finds published during the 19th century, unite them in a single work, and make them accessible to a wider public for the first time in a century. The new research has raised a series of questions about what might survive behind the sea wall at Meols, a topic which Silvia Gonzalez of Liverpool John Moores University is examining in detail.

The Meols project to catalogue the finds has been funded from a wide variety of sources, including the British Academy, the Aurelius Fund, the Millennium Award Sharing Museum Skills scheme, PH Holt Trust, the Roman Research Trust and Merseyside Archaeological Society. Grateful thanks are due to all of these bodies.

In 1846 the Revd Abraham Hume was visiting the parsonage in Hoylake, Wirral. He noticed some ancient artefacts, including a Roman brooch on the mantelpiece. Hume asked how they got there and learnt that local fishermen had found them on the shore at Meols. Realising the importance of the finds, he made efforts to recover further objects.

Meols, on the north Wirral coast, is now seen as one of the most significant ancient sites in the north west of England. For thousands of years, people had made use of a natural harbour called the Hoyle Lake. This gave its name in modern times to Hoylake, the town which grew up nearby. During the early 19th century storms and high tides had progressively washed away occupation deposits from a succession of settlements along the north Wirral coast. In less than a hundred years the shore-line retreated nearly 500 metres at Dove Point. Metal items from these layers were deposited on the beach where they were later found.

The objects range from the Neolithic through to the 18th century. There is a strong emphasis on the later medieval period but also a remarkable group of Roman, Saxon and Viking artefacts. After Hume began to publicise the finds in the 1840s, the site came to the attention of antiquarians who competed for the 'produce of the Cheshire shore'. Many amassed considerable collections. It is estimated that over a fifty-year period well over 5000 objects were found. A selection of the finest was published by Revd Hume in 1863 in his remarkable book, 'Ancient Meols'. Over 3000 objects, including some illustrated by Hume, still survive in modern museum collections, spread between no fewer than six institutions.

Meols' importance through the ages was due to its coastal location beside the Hoyle Lake, a haven on the Irish Sea coast. The objects show that the port began to develop about 2400 years ago, during the Iron Age. Finds such as a silver tetradrachm (a coin) of Tigranes I of Armenia, minted in Syria in the 1st century BC and bronze coins of Augustus, suggest that there had been contacts with France and even the Mediterranean before the Roman occupation of Britain. It is probable that a major item of the trade was salt from the brine springs of southern Cheshire.

Reassessment of the Roman finds suggests military activity at Meols in the pre-Flavian period before the foundation of the fortress at Chester and perhaps a market function afterwards. During the Roman period, the port grew to be the largest settlement in Merseyside. Over 70 Roman brooches and 120 coins have been found. This shows that Meols was a busy trading community. Ships sailing up the west coast of Britain would have stopped off to pick up goods or raw materials and trade pottery and other items. The local people may have lived in circular wooden houses, as the remains of such houses were found on the shore in the late 19th century.17

With thanks to the Museum of Liverpool

---

17 Liverpool Museum

Caldy

Caldy

In 1086 Caldy was part of the Manor of Calders which is an old Anglo Saxon word meaning "Cold Arse", named after a hill. It alluded to the prominent hill on which lie Grange and Caldy. It also gave its name to the hundred of Caldy, within the hundred of the Wirral. This is because all of the manors named as part of Caldy belonged to Robert Rhuddlan, Earl of Chester or the semi independent Norse colony permitted to settle there. Caldy is on the west side of the Wirral peninsula and is developed around the old village and Caldy manor which dates from the late 17th century. It was first mentioned in the Doomsday Book in 1086 as being owned by Hugh of Mere. Nearby is a large area of National Trust land called Caldy Hill. Many of the houses and walls are built from the local red sandstone.

To the North West, the village is bounded by the National Trust property known as Caldy Hill whilst the Dee estuary marks the western boundary of Caldy with more modern executive homes fringing the golf course. In 1832 the village was bought by a Mr R.W.Barton. A small public-house called the Hop Inn used to stand in the village. During the construction of the West Kirby to Hooton Railway in the 1880's the landlord of the Hop Inn, made a comfortable living by taking barrels of ale down to construction workers employed on the railway. The small inn later became a shop; this has now been converted into private house. At the turn of the 1900's, the village had a number of working farms, and the community was surrounded by open fields. The Manor House was occupied by James Ismay, whose father founded the White Star Line.

Development from 1906 to the late 1960s was by way of disposal of individual plots, in most instances for the purposes of the construction of single dwellings. The methods of sale continued to constitute a quite effective way of preserving the special character and nature of the Caldy village, which was one essentially of a low density area of good quality housing offering a high environmental quality. The Manor house was used for a time as a heart hospital in the 1950's. Today the building has been converted into flats. The majority of the village was designated a conservation area in October 1974 and only primarily residential use is permitted. At the time of the 2001 census, Caldy had 1,290 inhabitants, of a total ward population of 12,869.

Caldy Hill, West Kirby

Caldy Hill is an area of lowland heath and mixed deciduous woodland, located on a sandstone outcrop overlooking the Dee estuary. The area includes Stapledon Woods and lies to the south west side of Column Road (A540). Newton Common lies on the north side of Column Road and is small, mainly oak woodland. Grange Hill is located off Lang Lane, West Kirby and is an area of gorse and bracken scrub.

The whole area covers 250 acres of which 13 acres are owned by the National Trust. The hill and woodland can be reached by bus or train via West Kirby. Car parking is along Column Road or at Kings Drive North (see map). Horse riding is allowed on Fleck Lane and Kings Drive bridleway; it is also allowed around the periphery of Grange Hill. Cycling is permitted on the bridleways.

The hill rises to 260 ft. at its highest point where a view-finder stands. Fine views across the estuary and towards the Isle of Man

163

can be obtained in clear weather. The sandstone outcrop, on which the hill is located, is part of a ridge which extends from Heswall through Thurstaston and onto the Hilbre Islands.

Caldy Hill has a complex local history. All the land was acquired piecemeal by Hoylake District Council over the years between 1897 and 1974. Originally the hill was split up into small sections all privately owned by local landowners, and then given or sold with the understanding that the land was to be made open to the public and managed as countryside.

A major landmark is the Mariners Beacon which stands on the site of an old windmill. The mill was a very useful aid to maritime navigation and when it was destroyed by a gale in 1839, it was greatly missed. Consequently, the Trustees of the Liverpool Docks, with the permission of the landowner, Mr. Leigh, erected the Mariners Beacon in 1841.

Evidence of old enclosures can be seen on the hill in the form of old sandstone walls. Many of the older houses in the area are built from the stone taken from the quarries at Caldy and on Grange Hill. Some of these houses also have the original oak fences which were hand built by the carpenter of the Caldy Manor Estate, which previously owned much of the land in this area.

Evidence of old enclosures can be seen on the hill in the form of old sandstone walls. Many of the older houses in the area are built from the stone taken from the quarries at Caldy and on Grange Hill. Some of these houses also have the original oak fences which were hand built by the carpenter of the Caldy Manor Estate, which previously owned much of the land in this area.

The heath land is of regional significance with a variety of heathers including Ling, Cross-leaved and Bell Heather. The Gorse and Bracken with Birch and Oak scrub provide good cover for birds and small mammals. During the summer months insects and butterflies such as the Common Blue and Small Copper are present. Foxes use the bracken and bramble for cover during the day.

The oak trees on the heath are host to a variety of gall wasps. These insects lay their eggs in a specific part of the tree which responds by producing a gall, such as an Oak Apple in which the larva develops.

Stapledon Woods is a mixed plantation of Oak, Sweet Chestnut, Beech and Ash with Elm and Sycamore. During the spring the woods contain masses of Bluebells and Daffodils. Through the summer the trees support a variety of woodland birds such as Great Spotted and Lesser-spotted Woodpecker, Nuthatch and Tree creeper. Summer migrants include Spotted Flycatcher and warblers. Pied Flycatchers and Wood Warblers have started arriving in recent summers.

Caldy Parish Church

The building was originally an old school and part of Old Caldy Manor the date of construction is unknown. Since 1882 the building, of red sandstone, had been a chapel, converted from an outbuilding of Caldy Manor by Elizabeth Barton in memory of her husband Richard . It was decorated by C E Kempe, who designed several windows and added a clock turret. The church contains many memorials to the Bartons.

In 1893 the Manor passed to the Rev E A Waller, who added the north aisle and a saddle back tower. The building and its decoration windows, reredos, screen and other fittings; has an attractive unity of style, mainly from this single period. As the demands grew the building was extensively altered and north aisle, chancel and north east tower were added 1906 by Douglas and Minshull. Caldy Church was consecrated as the Church of the Resurrection and All Saints in 1907. The building is rock faced stone with ashlar dressings, slate roof with tile crest. The nave has a North aisle, baptistery, chancel north vestry and saddle-back tower.

The nave also has a gabled south porch and straight headed window of 3 cusped lights. The buttress marks can still be seen between the nave and choir, which has paired 2 light windows and end gabled buttress. The building also has a variety of mullioned windows and a large church tower which projects to east. Above entrance there is a lintel stone dated 1882. The choir stalls and altar rail have panels of marquetry and turned balusters. There is a tapering octagonal font with ribs and inscription; and a painted baptistery ceiling. The building also has some beautiful stained glass windows and a vestry fireplace with coat of arms, dated 1868. In the twentieth and twenty-first centuries the parishioners have continued to care devotedly for the church. It was refurbished in the 1960s, when the stalls and screens were painted in the present grey, white, gold and crimson. The black and white Hall seen above, built in 1883 as a studio, was bought from the Manor and fitted out by the parish in the 1970s.

The History of Caldy Rugby Club

Information taken from the Caldy RFC Website and I claim no credit as my own.

1924 – February 27th When some Old Boys of Calday School, with the encouragement of the then Headmaster, R. T. B. Glasspool, decided that they must carry on playing rugby together so the 'Old Caldeians' R.F.C. came into being at a meeting held at the Blenheim Café in West Kirby. They started playing in a farm field at Caldy cross roads and changing in the farm buildings at Croxton Farm, bathing facilities were somewhat primitive they used a tin bath which was filled from a tap in the farm Yard.

1925 - Sir Alfred Paton, an Old Boy of the school, bequeathed to The National Trust 20 acres land bordering Thurstaston Common with a proviso to the bequest stating that this area was to be available to the Rugby Club to use as a playing area in perpetuity. So Paton Field came into existence.

1928 – The club finally took possession of Paton Field and Built a Clubhouse with three changing rooms at a cost of £856-10-0. The club raised £400 in donations, £135 in loans, £ 130 in the form of guarantees and £100 from the RFU. This original clubhouse is still the core of the current clubhouse despite it being built mainly from wood.

1932 – The members held Summer camps where they spent their time levelling the 1st XV pitch in accordance with the terms of the lease, This took a number of summers and the original first team pitch was completed. This was under where the middle pitch is now.

1932 – Electricity was provided to the clubhouse with the help of boys from the school, who dug the trench from the main road to lay the cable. This also provided floodlights or training.

1933 – First Easter tour to Cumberland

1935 – In conjunction with the school the club held a summer Bazaar. The two-day event raised £600, which paid off the original dept from the clubhouse and further extensions.

1939-1945 The club continued to play Rugby during the war years with the support of the school and members who came back home on leave. During the conflict the club lost a number of members killed. JD.Thompson, the last pre war Captain was killed in Northern Ireland dealing with an unexploded bomb. J.Vanderverve, who played for the club when he was home, was killed in the Commando raid on St Nazaire. Many were killed in the North Africa campaign fighting with the Hoylake Horse Regiment.

1944 J.D. (Tommy) Thompson, a Master at Caldy who had played for the club since 1932, and other masters and members organised the first Sevens Competition at Paton Field. The event is now the Oldest continuously run Club Sevens in England. The profit from the first sevens competition was £12-7-0 and donated towards the cost of a war memorial at the club.

1946 – During the war the local farmer had been given grazing rights to the pitches at Paton Field. It was not until 1953 that the club were to resolve the matter and get the farmer off the pitches.

1947 – A schools 7's was incorporated into the annual sevens competition which ran until the 1970's when it was found that due to the changes in timetables many of the Local schools found it difficult to attend so it was dropped in 1975.

1947 – The club entered into negotiation with the National Trust to erect a stand. A fund was set up to pay for it.

1948 – The club built a bar at the club house and the gross profit for the first year was £75-4-8

1948 - 1949 The club won the Sevens competition both years.

1949 – A new first XV pitch was proposed and it was completed by 1953 and was officially opened for the 1953-4 season. Railings were put round the pitch, Mr J.B.Grier donated the piping and the members paid for the concrete posts. This is now the current Third pitch.

1951 – The Hoylake cricket club approached the Club with a view to moving to Paton Field; this was agreed subject to certain conditions.

1955 – The club drew up plans for a new extension to be built at the rear of the clubroom to house the new bar facilities, a kitchen, improved baths, a fireplace, and alterations to the changing rooms as well as a ladies toilet. The total coat of these improvements was £1230 plus the cost of the electrical work. The original bar was housed in the old Middle changing rooms and could not be opened until the players had finished changing. A master of the School and vice president of the club "Sammy" Watts excavated the cellar. The club obtained a loan from Inde & Coope Brewery for £255 for the bar fixtures and fittings and the Old Caldeian Union agreed to pay £900 for the fitting of the club room, which was to be called the "Memorial Hall" and the Roll of honour was to be placed above the fire place to commemorate the fallen in the second world war. The new hall was dedicated in 1957.

1959 – The entertainments organised the first major Sevens Dance on the Royal Iris and made a profit of £180.

1961 – The first Sevens dance was held at Paton Field featuring Humphrey Lyttelton and it was a great success making a profit of £572. This relieved the club of all its financial burdens and. A new development was planned to move the first XV pitch in front of the clubhouse. As the original land sloped gently down to the Cricket square it would require a substantial amount of land to be moved so it would have to be done by a professional company. The lowest tender came from Floods for £5953. This also involved using the surplus soil to raise the middle pitch and extend it towards the road. The club needed to raise a substantial sum of money but with the continued success of the sevens dances the club were able to proceed with the plan. To keep the cost down the club members dug up the posts round the old First XV pitch and replaced the round the new pitch and down the drive to the road. They also dug the steps up the bank to the clubhouse. The club with support of the Parkinson family purchased three sets of Metal posts to replace the old wooden ones. This was in memory of Eric Parkinson who died in 1966.

Sevens Dances - 1961 - Humphrey Lyttelton

1962 – Chris Barber

1963 – Kenny Ball

1964 – Acker Bilk

1965 – Humphrey Littleton

At the 1963 dance the club had booked a group called the Beatles on the undercard but they asked to be released as their record had just reached number one. The Four Pennies replaced them.

At the 1964 dance they attendance topped 4500 the main tent was over 100yds long and the bar tent 80yrds.

1964 – The club won £1000 on the premium bonds, which had been bought with the funds raised from the proposed Stand. It was agreed to invest this money and the Lottery win on the new ground.

1965 – The club approached the brewery with a view to building a lounge extension.

1966 - The club officially opened the new pitch on the 20th March with a game against a representative side comprising of players from the clubs who we had played in our fixture list.

1968 – The committee discussed the possibility of going "open" in view of the declining membership. An EGM was held on the 9th July when it was agreed to admit members who were not Old Boys of Calday School and the name of the club was changed from Old Caldeians to Caldy RFC.

1970 – Caldy became the first Junior club to win the Cheshire cup.

1970 – The Club won the Northern Old Boys Sevens and went on to play in the National Event in London. This was held at Richmond as a celebration of the Centenary to Rugby. The team won the Sunday Times Trophy in front of a large crowd against some of the largest rugby playing schools in the Country.

1971 – The club agreed to borrow £7000 from Higsons to finance the lounge extension and a further £2000 was needed to connect the club to the main sewerage system as it currently used a cesspit at the rear of the clubhouse. The club agreed that T.A.Parkinson (Meols) Ltd would build the extension but the members would keep the cost down by digging the footings. Modifications to the original was made to provide better changing rooms, re-equip the Kitchen, Re-site the Phone, and provide extra ladies toilets. This would cost a further £1500. The new lounge was officially opened in October.

1971 – In view of the increased administration required to maintain the clubhouse and grounds as well as managing the Bar. It was agreed that the Sections should amalgamate into one management committee with specific responsibility for the running of these rolls. The Caldy Club was formed.

1973 The club held a summer Carnival and raised £750

1974 – Mr Dai Adams formed a Mini Rugby Section at Caldy.

1975 – Mr Andrew Maxwell, a past member of the club, donated his England Shirt to the Club. It was a memento of the game he played against Australia in the recent Tour.

1978 – The club considered further development plans to increase the size of the lounge, add gent's toilets in the lounge area. It also would provide a Committee room and add 4 new dressing rooms to the end of the clubhouse. The club approached Higsons for a further loan for the lounge and The Sports Council for the Changing Rooms.

1980 – The club fielded 7 teams for the first time.

1982 – The club undertook it's second overseas tour where they took part in the Gent tournament; despite the lack of sleep they won the final and brought the Gent Cup Home.

1982 – The club agreed a loan from Higsons for a loan of £10,000 plus a grant of £4000 to be written off against barrelage. However the club needed to raise a deposit of £2,500. It was agreed to set up a fundraising committee. Selling Brick Certificates, Sponsored runs and lottery ticket sales raised the money. The fundraising kept up with and the work was finally completed in 1984 The total amount raised over the two years £10, 000. Work parties also helped to keep the cost of building the lounge extension and the Changing rooms down. The total cost of the improvements was £30,000 and the club only had to repay the Brewery loan of £10,000.

1983 – The Mini section continued to flourish but the senior sides were struggling and it was agreed that strenuous efforts needed to be made to turn the situation round.

1984 – The club obtained the services of a well-respected local coach Anthony Atherton and a 1st Team Manager Vic Baker.

1988 – The club won the Wirral Floodlight Cup

1988 – The club won the Taurus Floodlight Cup.

1988 – The club took part in the Giro Bank North West League Competition, which was the forerunner of National League Rugby.

1988 – We hosted a team from Paraguay, Curda, and made many friends. As a result of that trip we invited two of their players to return for the following season and experience English rugby. Both Players were International Players for Paraguay.

1988 – The first Team under the Captaincy of Roy Farebrother broke first team record for the number of wins and passed 1000 points fro the first time in the clubs history.

1990 – The Club consolidated the Mini and Junior sections and provided them with the same kit as the senior section. They were encouraged to organise themselves into committees and control their sections within the club.

1991 – The Sevens Committee added an international Sevens competition to the already successful Merseyside Sevens Competition. It proved a great success attracting many overseas sides, Fiji, Western Samoa, Russia, Latvia, Malaysia, together with representative sides from Canada, South Africa, France and Scotland. A number of top English sides also took part, including Harlequins Wasps, Orrell, Bristol and many more. One notable young player for the Wasps side was Lawrence Dallaglio. However with the advent of professional Rugby this event had to be dropped, as we were unable to compete with the bigger sponsored events that were set up in competition. The event is still held in esteem as one of the best-run events on the calendar. And its hospitality was legendary.

1996 – The club were runners up on the North West 3 league and were promoted to North West 2.

1997 - The club won North West 2 League and were promoted again. This was the first league title for the club since the start of league Rugby.

2003 - The club needed to rebuild after a disastrous last season and re appointed Anthony Atherton as Director of Rugby to oversee the restructuring of the paying side from first XV through to the Mini section. Concentrating on the strength of our current youth and Mini sections rather than looking outside for players rebuilt the first xv Squad was the key to the sub sequential success of the club. The Club won the league title and were successful in getting back to North 2 West at the first time of asking. The 2nd XV also had a successful season scoring over 1000 points. The colts did the double winning their league and Cup competitions. The club was the 5th club in England to be awarded the RFU "Seal of Approval" and Sports Match Accreditation. It was recognised by Wirral and awarded Sports club of the Year. It also won the Merseyside Sports "Community Club" of the Year and the prestigious Rugby World Magazine "Team Of The Year" in competition with all other clubs in the UK and Ireland.

2004 – The Club were Runners up in North 2 West and just lost out in the play off away at Middlesborough 21-13. The 2nd XV were runners up in the inaugural Fairclough Homes 2nd XV League to Macclesfield. The Colts got to the last 8 in the National knock out competition and won their league and Cheshire Cup for the second time. The Club also achieved Year 2 Status with the

RFU seal of Approval development plan and were the first club in England to achieve this.

2005 – The club were champions of North 2 West and were promoted for the first time to North 1, Level 5 in the pyramid in The English League Structure and meant that they were now one of the top 120 clubs in the English leagues. During that season the Senior Colts were runners up in the Cheshire Cup and the Junior Colts won their league. The under 15 Scored over 1500 points in the season and the Mini section increased their membership to over 180 and they won two of the 5 Cheshire Tournaments.

Bibliography

1 William Webb, 1622

2 A Perambulation of the Hundred of Wirral. Harold Edgar Young, 1909

3 Ferguson Irvine, Village Life in West Kirby 300 years ago, 1895

4 John Brassie

5 *www.hilbrebirdobs.co.uk*

6 *www.deeestuary.co.uk*

7 Gentleman's Magazine June, 1796

8 Harold Edgar Young, A Perambulation of the Hundred of Wirral, 1909

9 Iter-Lancastrense, 1636

10 Philip Sulley, 1889

11 E.W Cox, 1895

12 David Griffiths, *British Archaeology magazine (December 2001).*

13 Wirral Globe, Friday 25th June, 2010

14 Prof Stephen Harding

15 Peter France & John Emmett

16 Peter France & John Emmett

17 Liverpool Museum

This Page intentionally left blank

This Page intentionally left blank

Printed in Great Britain
by Amazon.co.uk, Ltd.,
Marston Gate.